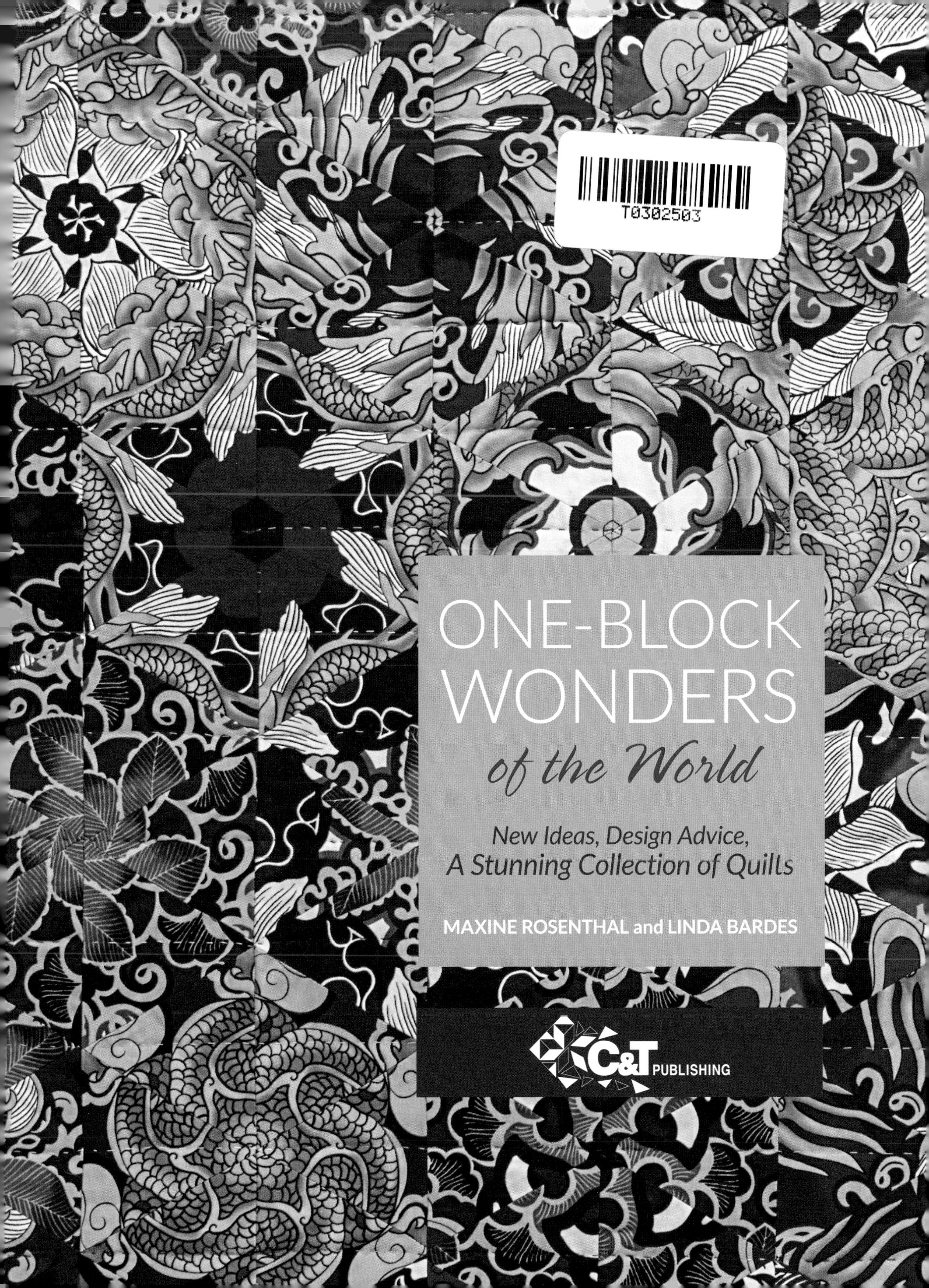

ONE-BLOCK WONDERS

of the World

New Ideas, Design Advice,
A Stunning Collection of Quilts

MAXINE ROSENTHAL and LINDA BARDES

C&T PUBLISHING

Publisher: Amy Marson

Creative Director: Gailen Runge

Editors: Karla Menaugh and Liz Aneloski

Technical Editor: Debbie Rodgers

Cover Designer: April Mostek

Book Designer: Christina Jarumay Fox

Production Coordinator: Tim Manibusan

Production Editors: Alice Mace Nakanishi and Jennifer Warren

Photo Assistant: Mai Yong Vang

Photography by Diane Pedersen of C&T Publishing, Inc., unless otherwise noted

Published by C&T Publishing, Inc., P.O. Box 1456, Lafayette, CA 94549

Library of Congress Cataloging-in-Publication Data

Names: Rosenthal, Maxine, 1944- author. | Bardes, Linda, 1943- author.

Title: One-block wonders of the world : new ideas, design advice, a stunning collection of quilts / Maxine Rosenthal and Linda Bardes.

Description: Lafayette, CA : C&T Publishing, Inc., 2017.

Identifiers: LCCN 2017013882 | ISBN 9781617455186 (soft cover)

Subjects: LCSH: Patchwork--Patterns. | Quilting.

Classification: LCC TT835 .R6744 2017 | DDC 746.46--dc23

LC record available at https://lccn.loc.gov/2017013882

Printed in the USA

10 9 8 7 6 5

ACKNOWLEDGMENTS

We want to acknowledge all of the One Block Wonder Quilt Forum members on Facebook. You have inspired us from the beginning with all of the unique quilts you have posted and continue to post on the forum. You took Maxine's basic process and innovated in unforeseen yet brilliant ways that stimulated the idea for this book. We are only sorry that we were unable to use many of the quilts from artists who wanted to contribute to this project. We made our choices based on the story we wanted to tell, not because we thought one quilt was better than another. Thank you.

DEDICATION

To One-Block Wonder artists everywhere, who have created so many amazing and one-of-a-kind quilts.

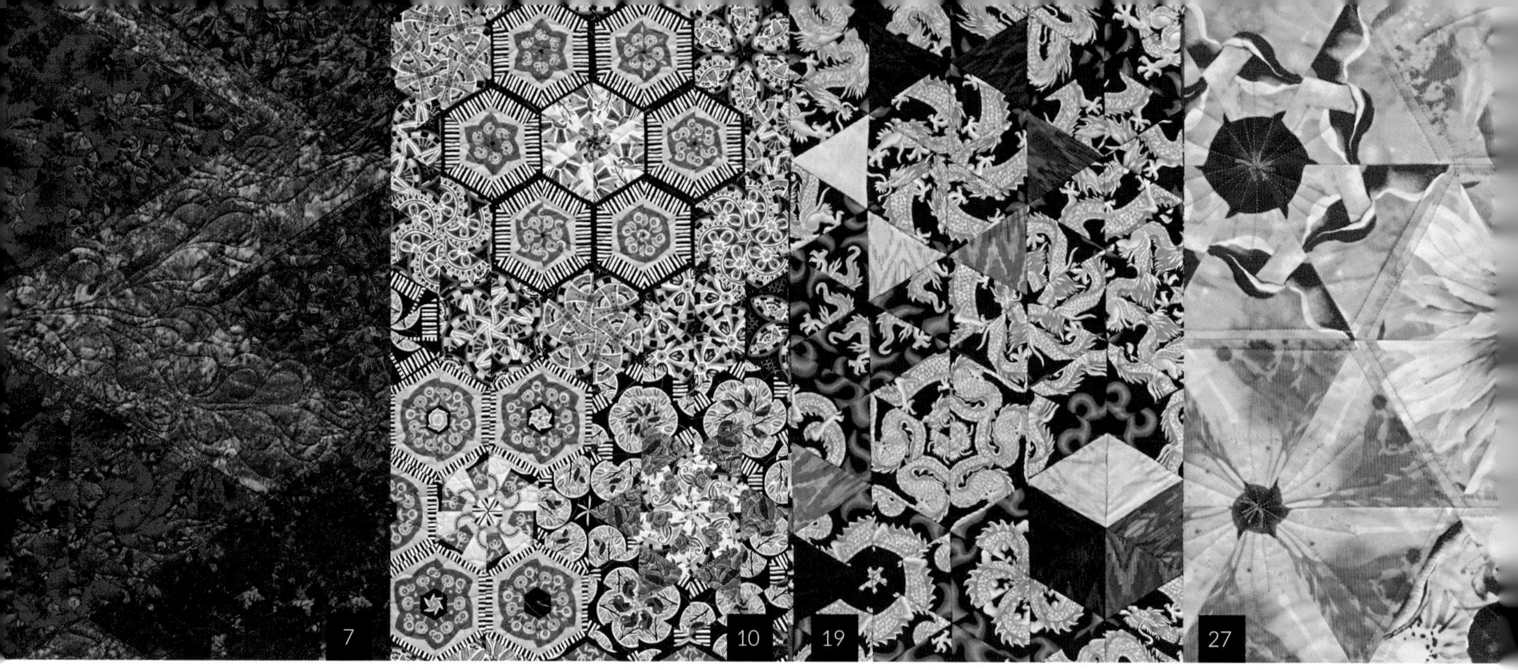

CONTENTS

34

47

53

73

FOREWORD

LINDA SAYS:

I came late to quilting, even though I have been sewing since I was 12. I am now 74. My retirement began when I was 60, and I floundered for a while until I started sewing little purses and bags.

After watching Nancy Zieman interview Bruce Seeds about his One-Block Wonder (OBW) quilts, I was smitten. YouTube videos further excited me. I bought two of Maxine Rosenthal's One-Block Wonder books and began to sew my own One-Block Wonders (OBWs).

Even though I was not enthusiastic about traditional quilts or even modern quilts, I liked OBWs because I did not need to have a stash of fabric to create them. One fabric, plus any borders I might want, was all that I needed. I also liked that with these quilts, what you see is *not* what you get. The mystery and the process seduced me.

Shortly after I sewed my first OBW using an upholstery fabric, I looked for an OBW group on Facebook but did not find one. So I created the One Block Wonder Quilt Forum. Within a year there were more than 3,000 members, and after a year and a half, there were almost 5,000 members from all over the world.

Maxine and I have seen some amazingly beautiful and unique quilts. People were using Maxine's basic instructions and process to innovate all over the place. Members were creating and sharing how-to files, creating photo albums, and responding intelligently and respectfully to questions. One day I noticed that Maxine Rosenthal had commented on someone's question, so I sent her a message suggesting that there was enough material in the group for a fourth book. "Why don't you help me do it?" she responded. That had not been my intention, but I recognized it as an opportunity. Who would have guessed that we both lived in the same city?

I put together a table of contents and sent it to Maxine. I think about the phrase, "Chance favors the prepared mind." It was as though we were waiting for what happened next. Maxine was contacted by C&T Publishing to see if she had any ideas for another book. We sent in the table of contents, our proposal was accepted, and here we are—writing *One-Block Wonders of the World*.

Magic, pure magic!

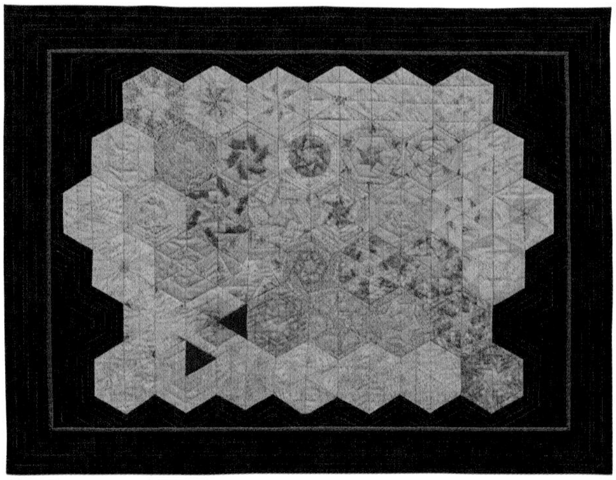

***Joy/Luck*, 42″ × 38″, machine pieced and quilted by Linda Bardes, 2013. Pieced using 3¾″ strips.**

This is my first One-Block Wonder quilt. Right from the beginning, I called it Joy/Luck. *Little did I know that this quilt would create exactly that!*

CHAPTER

1

INTRODUCTION

This book began as a Facebook page—the One Block Wonder Quilt Forum. Making a One-Block Wonder is a process, a technique that is open to interpretation and application. A One-Block Wonder is not made from a pattern; that is its beauty and its frustration. It is about living in the mystery. That mystery is what keeps quilters coming back again and again.

The focus of this book is to offer design help, to show you what others have done (the beginning fabric and the ending project), and to empower you to cut into that beautiful fabric that has been sitting in the closet.

We'll show you many before and after photos, because one of the most asked questions on the online forum is, "Will you show the original fabric?" (We include the fabric manufacturer's information, too, if available.) It is amazing what is produced from each fabric. Often we would never have guessed that a certain fabric would produce such a quilt.

People have taken the basic concepts of a One-Block Wonder, played with them, and invented their own ideas. This book is about sharing those ideas with you. This book, then, is about *your* creations with the One-Block Wonder technique. You have so many more ideas than we alone could possibly have. This book is a tribute to everyone who has added to the One-Block Wonder experience.

The original book, *One-Block Wonders* (by C&T Publishing), included hexagons and octagons. This book will focus only on hexagons, since that is what most people are using. We give you as much information about each quilt as the artist could supply, but some completion dates are not known, nor are all the details about the fabrics.

A hexagon is a six-sided object. A One-Block Wonder block is a hexagon composed of six identical equilateral triangles that form a kaleidoscopic image. The hexagons are then put on the design wall with no space between them and moved around and around until a pleasing design is created. With just a few borders, a quilt is complete. One fabric, one quilt. The basic construction is simple—no Y-seams—but for most people, the challenge is in the design.

SUPPLIES

You will need just a few basic supplies—a rotary cutter and mat, a ruler, flower-head pins, a sewing machine, and a design wall.

The Differences in 60° Rulers

The 60° line on a rectangular ruler is enough to cut all the triangles, but you might find it easier to use a 60° triangle ruler. There are several 60° rulers available, and there seem to be two styles—one that has a point and one that does not have a point. *There is a difference between the two.*

MAXINE SAYS:

When I started making One-Block Wonders, there was one 60° triangle ruler style available. The ruler had a point at the end, and measuring down the center of the triangle began right at that tip. Now there is another style of 60° ruler, one without a tip. Measuring down the center begins at that cut-off edge, which is ¼″ away from what would have been the point. When you lay each ruler with the 3¾″ line along the bottom of a 3¾″ strip of fabric, you have two different triangle sizes. In reality you have a triangle and a trapezoid. That means that a triangle cut with the 3¾″ line on the ruler with the point is not the same as a triangle cut with the 3¾″ line of the ruler without the point. For the triangles to be the same size, you would have to place the ruler without the point on the 3½″ line, because the missing tip is ¼″.

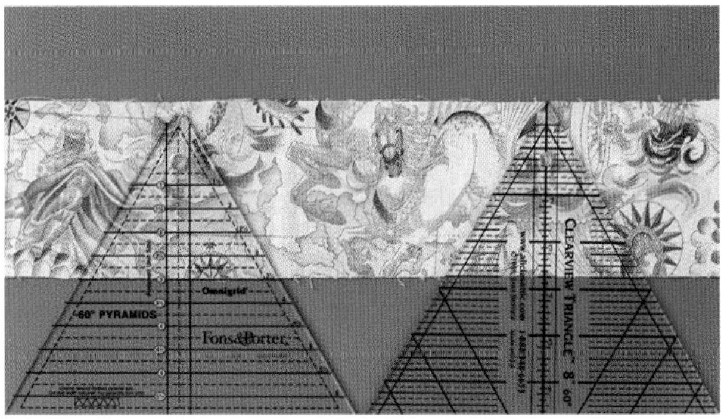

When you place both rulers on the 3¾″ mark, the triangle cut from the ruler without the point will be wider. Move the ruler without the point to the 3½″ mark.

Design Wall

A design wall is not a necessity. It is helpful, however, because working on the floor, a bed, or a table distorts the perspective, color, and size of the blocks, which in turn makes it harder to design.

MAXINE SAYS:

I covered an entire wall with a sheet of insulation and covered that with cotton batting. Cotton fabric tends to stick to this batting, so I need only push blocks to the wall and they stick, making it easy to move the blocks around as I design. I can also push a pin straight into the insulation without damaging the wall.

LINDA SAYS:

Because I have the space, I covered an entire wall with felt, using pushpins to hold it in place. It seems to grip almost any fabric I use. Hint: If you have an open window next to your wall, don't leave it open on a windy day!

Pins

For cutting, we like to use flower-head pins for pinning the fabric layers together. These pins lie flat and do not shift as you cut. And the rulers do not shift as you cut. With regular pins, the ruler is likely to wobble, causing uneven strips that then make for uneven hexagons . . . and frustration.

MAXINE SAYS:

I use regular straight pins when pinning the half-hexagons together; by then it doesn't matter. Straight pins are cheaper than flower-head pins, and flower-head pins would stand out on the wall.

LINDA SAYS:

I like to use the flower-head pins for almost everything, because they are extra long and easy to pick up. I do not notice the pins in the hexagons on the wall. Flower-head pins can be expensive and do not last as long as regular straight pins, however.

CHAPTER

2

SOME THOUGHTS ON CHOOSING FABRIC

BASIC GUIDELINES

Choosing fabric may seem like a daunting task, but with a One-Block Wonder (OBW), you choose only one fabric to create a fabulous quilt. Here are a few guidelines that may be helpful.

- Do not use batik fabric or any hand-printed fabric. The repeats will not match up.
- If you like the color of the fabric, you will like the quilt. Big, bright orange flowers will always produce an orange quilt, so if you choose a fabric with big, bright orange flowers, we hope you like orange.
- The larger the elements within the design, the less the finished quilt will look like the original fabric.
- The less background in the print, the better. There should be less background than pattern.
- Fabrics with animals are great—you get hexagons of all eyes or all tails. Fun for kids of all ages.
- Try to limit the number of colors in the fabric. Using too many colors makes designing more difficult. Some OBW quilters think that four colors or tones are enough.
- Try to avoid fabrics with straight lines that run parallel or perpendicular to the selvage. When you sew the triangles together, your eye will want those lines to match exactly. Shapes that curve do not need to match from one triangle to another.
- A design that repeats often is not as interesting as a design with a variety of flowers or other elements. Note that the design may repeat along the selvage as well as from selvage to selvage. When the repeat occurs in both directions, it could take only half of the yardage you might expect to get six repeats, because three repeats will be on one side of the fold and three on the other side.
- Some backgrounds are a solid color; others may have a pattern, such as a swirl. The ones with some variation will make the quilt more interesting.
- A fabric with a black background will produce a much more intense quilt than one with a beige background. The question is, what are you looking for in a quilt? What colors do you like? Are you looking for drama? Choosing a fabric with a black background is a sure way to uncover and feature a bold design.

With that said, you will see quilts in which the quiltmakers ignored some of the guidelines, and still the quilt is stunning. For example, see *Life, the Universe, and Everything* (page 14), wherein Bruce Seeds used fabric with straight lines to make a wonderful quilt.

HOW MUCH FABRIC TO BUY?

You should determine how much fabric you need by looking at the repeat of the design rather than at the yardage. You can recognize a repeat by looking along the length of the fabric to see where a design element appears again. Smaller repeats tend to have smaller elements.

Since hexagons are made of six triangles, you will need six repeats of the design to create the hexagons for any quilt. And you might consider buying an extra ½ yard so that you can put a little of the original fabric on the back of the quilt, just to show where you started. If you want to use some original fabric in a border, buy an extra yard of fabric.

LENGTH OF REPEAT	× 6 REPEATS	YARDAGE NEEDED	+ ½ YARD FOR THE BACK	YIELDS NUMBER OF HEXAGON BLOCKS
8″	48″	1⅓ yards	1⅞ yards	36–38
12″	72″	2 yards	2½ yards	54–57
16″	96″	2⅔ yards	3¼ yards	72–76
24″	144″	4 yards	4½ yards	108–114

MAXINE SAYS:

The final size of the quilt depends on the design process, how many hexagons and/or cubes are used, whether you add borders, and so on. To give you a rough idea, 2 yards of a 12″ repeat will make a baby-size quilt. Using 4 yards of a fabric with a 24″ repeat, I will get a good lap-size quilt—maybe 60″ × 70″. I have also made a large queen-size quilt using 4½ yards and lots of cubes and borders.

hint

To make a larger quilt, you can always double the yardage. For example, if you have a 12″ repeat and purchase 4 yards for the blocks instead of the 2 yards shown in the chart, you would have the same number of blocks as a 24″ repeat. If you are making a king-size quilt, you might need 8 yards of a 24″ repeat, plus the ½ yard for fabric to include on the back.

USING PANELS

Panels are interesting to work with. You will find many drawbacks, however. First, panels usually are banded in black. You may choose to use the black bands in your design; they can create some interesting pinwheels. Or you may cut them off before you cut your strips.

Second, you will often find a lot of open areas with one color in a panel that may have little relationship to the other hexagons when assembled. These can end up being one-of-a-kind. This makes designing a challenge because it is difficult to develop a flow in the overall design, but that very challenge creates some very dynamic and interesting works of art. Just be aware that working with panels is very different from working with a fabric that has an allover design with repeating colors and patterns. Some of the most unlikely panels, however, can result in unexpected awesomeness. See Preprinted Panels (page 65) for some examples.

FABRICS THAT SHOULDN'T HAVE WORKED BUT DID

There are some fabrics that do not work well, but then again, they just might....

We have seen fabulous One-Block Wonders made from fabric that we would never consider a possibility. They began with the most unlikely of fabric designs, and yet magic resulted. Later in this chapter, we'll show you some fabrics that from all appearances should not have worked, along with the quilts that were created as a result of the rebel eye of the quilter. A good many of the quilts in this book actually don't follow the original guidelines we've presented.

You may want to keep this in mind, however:

- With a repeat in which all the elements of the design—especially the color and pattern—are densely repetitive, you will have lots of hexagons that look the same, making it hard to find a layout.
- A fabric with only a few soft, muted colors and a large neutral background will create a layout design with very little character and not very much, but some, potential.
- A fabric with little or no background creates hexagons that often look like the original fabric.

You will find some examples of such fabrics in this book. What you also will notice is that they are all what we refer to as design opportunities. By adding other elements, such as cubes or complementary fabrics or other colorways, beauty pours out where there was little before!

MAXINE SAYS:

Stay away from fabrics with lines that run parallel or perpendicular to the selvage—when you sew them together, you will need to match those straight lines. My aim is to avoid having to be very careful about my sewing. I tend to like fabrics with bold colors and black backgrounds, but that is a choice. Light or limited colors, or several colors of the same intensity, are not my choice, nor are narrow (4″) repeats.

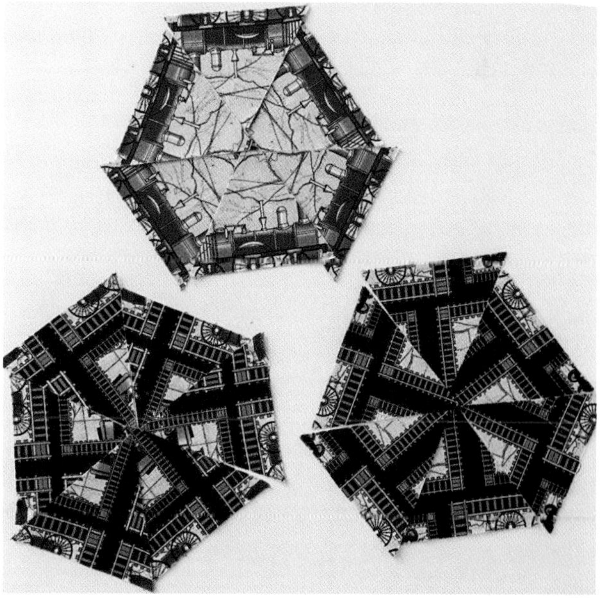

Hexagons in which lines do not match

However ...

QUILTS WHERE IGNORING THE GUIDELINES WORKED

Photo by Bruce Seeds

***Life, the Universe, and Everything*, 95″ × 90″, machine pieced by Bruce Seeds, machine quilted by Diane Minkley for Patched Works, Inc., 2016. Pieced using 3¾″ strips.**

"I usually don't name my quilts until I have completed the layout. However, since this was the forty-second quilt I created, I took the title from The Hitchhiker's Guide to the Galaxy, *by Douglas Adams. According to Adams, the answer to the ultimate question of 'life, the universe, and everything' is '42.' I first began by laying out the hexagons in the shape of a gentle curve, but I didn't like that and removed all of them. I organized them on my worktable in a series of color gradients and returned them to the wall. The result looks almost three-dimensional from certain angles, but the quilt is flat."*

Photo by Bruce Seeds

This is the first layout Bruce tried with his Alexander Henry fabric. He later scrapped this layout for the final design of *Life, the Universe, and Everything*.

Photo by Bruce Seeds

Original fabric for *Life, the Universe, and Everything*: Prairie House by Alexander Henry. The repeat is approximately 24″. This fabric has straight lines, which typically cause challenges for OBW quilts.

LINDA SAYS:

I'm not a very good student. In spite of the 25 times or more that I paged through and read Maxine's first 2 books, I simply bought the fabric I liked. My first piece, *Joy/Luck* (page 6), was made from an upholstery fabric with a repeat that was printed entirely in shadings of gold, brown, and gray. My next was an Asian fabric that was more of a panel and had a lot of blank space. It wasn't until I cut it that I realized the open space created a lot of plain hexagons. I did not use many of them.

Even now, after creating several One-Block Wonders, I still tend to choose what I like. Which is slightly—well, let's face it—sometimes it's *very* far left or right of the guidelines.

What I am able to do at this stage of experience is know what I'm getting into. I recognize that there are many design opportunities in all fabrics. Some fabrics just take a little more time to tease out a pleasing layout. Since I don't sell my quilts, I don't care how long it takes to complete one.

If you are new to this process, look carefully at the finished quilts and the original fabrics and try to match the guidelines with each fabric. Then take the book with you when you go shopping. After you have made one or two One-Block Wonders and are familiar with the basic process of cutting and pinning and sewing and designing, live dangerously!

"I was told by some OBW makers that this fabric would not work because it had too much plain background, but I thought, 'Oh well, nothing to lose.' As I cut my strips, I trimmed them in places to get variety and to use as much of the color sections as possible. After I was happy with the design, I cut all of the remaining hexagons down for the borders and had none left over."

Original fabric for *Shoe Shuffle*. Faye used the fabric on the back of the quilt.

***Shoe Shuffle*, 57½″ × 57½″, machine pieced and quilted by Faye McCarthy. Pieced using 3¾″ strips.**

Gardens of the Galaxy, 73″ × 84″, machine pieced and quilted by Sharon H. Lake. Pieced using 3¼″ strips.

"I chose this fabric because I love the colors, and I wanted something that would give me several hexagons that were alike or very similar. I love the millefiori quilts and thought I could make an OBW that was in the millefiori style. I also used all the little half-triangles that were left at the ends of the strips, since I am very frugal. Sometimes I sewed two halves from the main fabric together, and sometimes I used half from the main fabric and half from an accent fabric. I like the little spinning stars that result from doing this."

Detail of *Gardens of the Galaxy*. The spinning stars appear where Sharon sewed half-triangles together to make the full triangles for some of the hexagons.

Original fabric for *Gardens of the Galaxy*: Round the Garden by Mary Engelbreit for Andover Fabrics, Inc.

Photo by Lisa Fritz of Camralynz Photography

Super Nova, 94″ × 70¾″, machine pieced and quilted by Darlene Williams.
Pieced using 3¾″ strips.

Photo by Lisa Fritz of Camralynz Photography

Original fabric for *Super Nova*: April Showers Bring Sunflowers by George Mendoza for FreeSpirit Fabric. The repeat is 17″.

"I made an impulse buy of three or four yards of this fabric in 2010. When I saw my first OBW at a quilt show in Waco, Texas, in 2015, I was mesmerized by what I saw and knew that I already had the perfect fabric. With the encouragement of my friend Tabatha Smith, I designed the center of the quilt and then the surrounding layout. Many hexagons were left over, and they were conveniently arranged on my design wall in a sort of border. I saw what to do with the border immediately. I quilted it in an allover loop design with variegated thread. A friend named the quilt Super Nova *because she thought it looked as if a star was exploding."*

April in Paris, 35″ × 24″, machine pieced and quilted by May Smith. Pieced using 3¾″ strips.

"This quilt will eventually become a sewing-machine cover. I echo quilted around each block with variegated thread to keep the focus on the beautiful blocks."

Photo by May Smith

Original fabric for *April in Paris*: Paris by Timeless Treasures

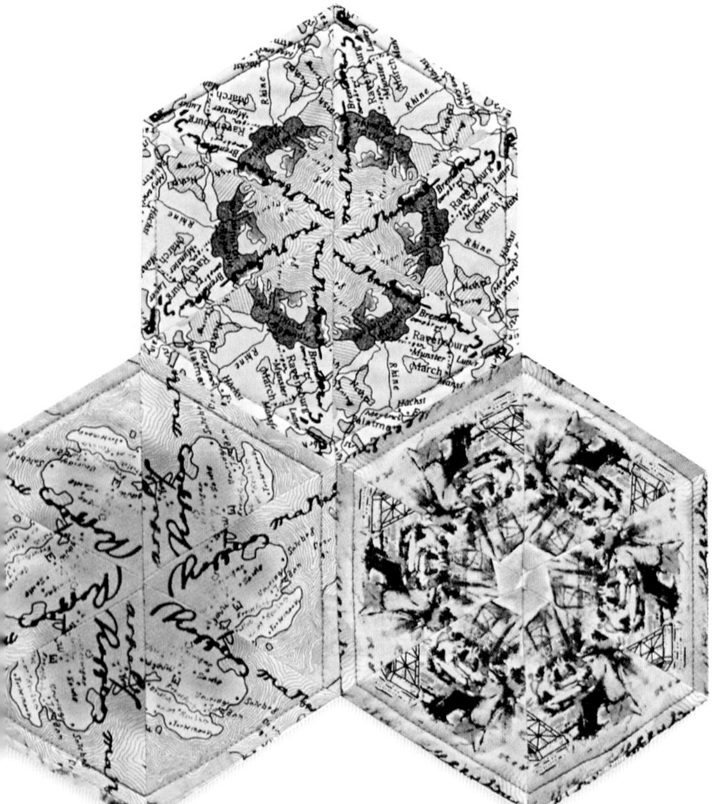

CHAPTER

3

CUTTING AND SEWING

For a comprehensive look at how to identify repeats in your fabric, cut strips and triangles for the hexagons, and assemble a One-Block Wonder quilt, see the previous books in this series: *One-Block Wonders*, *One-Block Wonders Encore!*, and *One-Block Wonders Cubed!* (all by C&T Publishing). The books contain a wealth of instructional information, and we couldn't possibly repeat it all here. What follows are the answers to some of our most frequently asked questions from the Facebook page and some updated techniques for making One-Block Wonder quilts.

HOW WIDE SHOULD I CUT THE STRIPS?

MAXINE SAYS:

I began making these quilts by cutting the strips 3¾″ wide. It was simple math for me. Most printed fabric prints have some multiple of a 4″ repeat, which means that the repeat is divisible by four, such as a 24″ repeat, an 8″ repeat, or even a 16″ repeat. As I was looking for repeats to cut, 4″ would be the perfect beginning. But that would assume that I would cut perfectly each time, which is not me, so I gave myself ¼″ for inaccuracy. That is how I came up with 3¾″ strips. That number has turned out to be a stroke of genius because it is easily divided by three, which is what is needed for the cubes. *One-Block Wonders Encore!* or *One-Block Wonders Cubed!* has information on all the varieties of cubes.

The fact is that the strips can be any size. I have tried other sizes, and I keep coming back to 3¾″. I've found that the smaller the strip, the more sewing you need to do to make a smaller quilt, and the larger the strip, the more the hexagon looks like the original fabric.

If you cut six layers of a 3¾″ strip across the width of fabric, you will have enough triangles to make eighteen or nineteen kaleidoscopic hexagons. This gives you plenty to play with later. Each strip that you cut produces a different array of kaleidoscopic effects, possibly even different colors, depending on your fabric.

LINDA SAYS:

Any size works. I have no preconceived notions, and I don't obsess about getting the most out of these layered panels. If I have wide enough strips left after I'm done, I can use them for binding, or they go in a box for future use.

I have, however, developed a technique that helps me decide how wide to cut my strips, especially with a challenging fabric. I take two strips of paper and lay the first strip close to one edge of the uncut fabric.

Place the first strip close to the uncut edge.

I lay the second strip of paper parallel to and about 3¾″ away from the first. As I move the papers back and forth and up and down, I can watch the design elements in the fabric and change the width between the strips.

Move the paper strips around on the fabric.

I also add paper triangle cutouts to get an even better idea. I may decide to cut an inch or two off the fabric, creating a new edge before I cut all six strips. Once I have cut, I don't look back.

Use more paper strips to look at triangle possibilities.

This also gives me a good idea as to how large to cut the strips. For instance, with the fabric below, I wanted to make the hexagons larger so that I would not have so many that were just a plain color, such as the orange or red. For that reason, I cut them 4¼″.

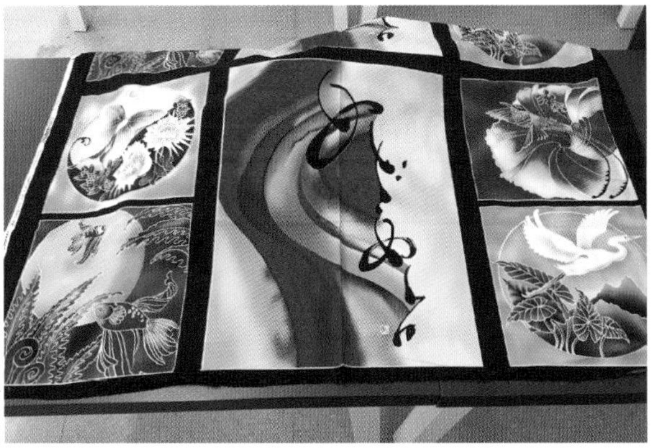

Photo by Linda Bardes

This panel, the starting place for *Tropical Sunset* (page 66), had large areas of orange and red.

Photo by Linda Bardes

To help me figure out how wide to cut the strips, I used white rectangles and open triangles to audition various strip sizes.

We have seen many quilts now for which people cut strips at widths other than 3¾″, and they are fantastic quilts. The bottom line is that this is your quilt; all the decisions are yours.

Some people question whether to cut the width of the fabric in half down the fold. If you do that, you have wasted one hexagon on each strip. That may not sound like much, but those hexagons are probably the very ones you will need when designing the whole quilt. The decision is entirely up to you.

SEWING HEXAGONS TOGETHER

The same triangles arranged three ways

MAXINE SAYS:

I never look at the placement possibilities of the triangles.

The reality is that they are equilateral triangles and can be arranged three different ways. If you look at each possibility and decide on the one you like the best, it takes a very long time to sew.

The other reason I don't do this is that your eye favors the pattern to be in the center of the hexagon, but that does not always make the hexagons play well together.

This is a serendipitous approach. For me this means that the surprise comes as you press, which adds interest to what I consider a dull task. Designing is the best part of this process, and I want to get there as quickly as possible.

LINDA SAYS:

I love playing with each hexagon before I sew. This is the part I like best. I lovingly audition each possibility of triangle arrangement and don't pay any attention to the straight of grain. I can always unsew and rearrange later if I need a different arrangement to help create the ultimate design. Somehow it always works out in the end.

Sew the triangles into half-hexagons and remember to *always* press the seams open. *Note: Do not sew the halves together.* Instead, pin each hexagon together with the edge of one half overlapping the edge of its mate. This allows the hexagons to lie flat on the design wall.

Pinned blocks. Do not sew the hexagon halves together.

Start putting them on the wall to see how they look, and admire as you go. Keep in mind that you cannot design the entire quilt until all the blocks are there.

WHAT IF I DON'T HAVE SIX REPEATS?

Not to worry. It is simply a "design opportunity."

A hexagon is six sided; there is no way around that. But what would happen if you made half-hexagons and instead of pinning each together with its mate, you matched them to others? What if you used a triangle from another hexagon to complete the six or added another fabric altogether? Resourcefulness changes the layout, but that is what is called a *design opportunity.*

Hexagons made with six identical triangles

A hexagon made with one different triangle

The same hexagons made by switching halves

Mix it up even more! These hexagons meld together by using five triangles for each.

MAXINE SAYS:

Since you are using half-hexagons, you can sew your quilt together in straight lines, in a column, or a row at a time.

As you sew the columns together, you will notice that the points from the triangles all begin to line up, especially as you match the center of the hexagon.

The half-hexagons make it possible to sew the quilt in straight lines.

The points line up as you sew.

LINDA SAYS:

I picked up this fabric at a huge tag sale. It was labeled four yards, but it turned out to be 4″ short. The pattern was 24½″, which made the sixth repeat even shorter. Here's how I handled this shortage.

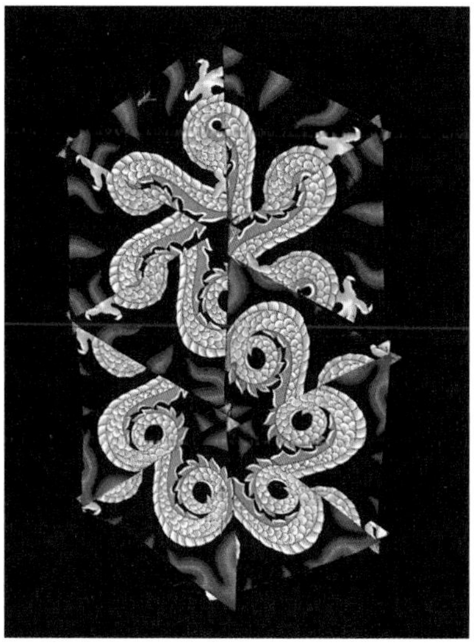

Photo by Linda Bardes

Twins: Since each hexagon is missing one triangle, they tuck up neatly inside each other.

Photo by Linda Bardes

By using a star surround, you automatically fill in the empty space. Watch where you line up your empty spaces. See Hint (page 24).

Photo by Linda Bardes

Here is a basic layout using many different fill-in techniques. How many can you find?

hint

I did not sew any half-hexagons together when constructing the main body of Dragons on Parade. *Instead, I placed triangles one at a time, thinking it would be easier than taking apart any sewn half-hexagons to replace a triangle with the odd fabric.*

What a mess I had when I sewed the triangles together in strips! I had made so many mistakes that it took forever to rip and sew, rip and sew. After it was all finished, I noticed another mistake! It's still there.

My advice? Design as usual with half-hexagons. Lay the new fabric triangle on top as you design, then selectively remove the triangle under it and replace it with the new one when you have finalized your design. It will be a bit of a nuisance but not nearly as much of an aggravation as the way I did it!

Dragons on Parade, 45″ × 60½″, machine pieced and quilted by Linda Bardes, 2016. Pieced using 3¾″ strips.

"I knew there would be a lot of waste with this fabric, so I carefully chose where to trim the beginning edge of my repeats so I could get as much of the yellow/orange in the strips as possible. Since the fabric pattern consisted almost entirely of dragons, I decided to name the quilt Dragons on Parade, *and I sketched out a preliminary layout that featured the dragons marching across two of the borders. I could see right away that I needed to run a thin ¼″ border to feature the layout. But what color, yellow or blue? And what would be the best binding? I did not have enough fabric left over to finish the quilt. I auditioned colors by printing out pictures of the layouts, pasting the pictures on paper, and playing with colored pencils until I liked what I saw. I appliquéd the dragons to the finished quilt."*

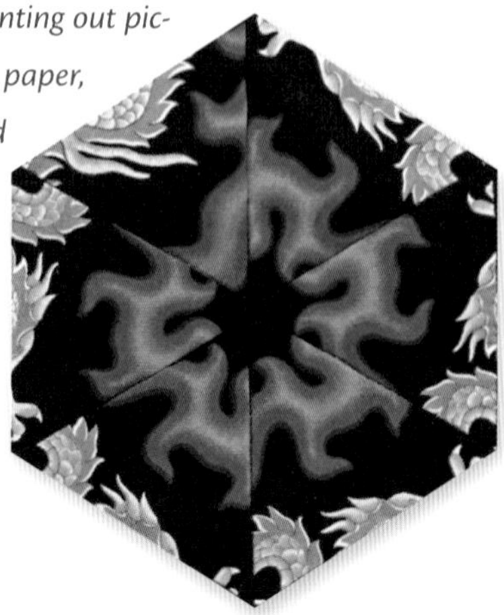

Birds in the Garden, 42″ × 32½″, machine pieced and quilted by Linda Bardes. Pieced using 2¾″ strips.

hint

Fussy cutting can be a useful tool in making a One-Block Wonder. Fussy cutting means thoughtfully cutting to get something specific from your fabric. You can fussy cut strips, throwing away a thin strip or two to get exactly what you want. You can even fussy cut the triangles from the strips to feature a specific pattern or color. If you need a particular color or pattern to balance your design and there isn't a hexagon left that will work, you can cut a full hexagon from your leftover fabric. You will have some Y-seams to sew, but it will be worth it if you get the look you want. When I made Birds in the Garden, *using whole hexagons helped me resolve design issues. For another quilt that features fussy-cut whole hexagons, see* Girl Dreaming of Kaleidoscopes and Tumbling Blocks *(page 65).*

**"It turned out that many of my hexagons were so alike and so busy that something was missing from the layout. So I fussy cut two whole hexagons of birds, and I had my story. Yet the balance was still off. I needed a few more white blocks. I fussy cut two whole white flowers out of the leftovers, and that solved the problem. With the whole hexagons in the quilt, I had to sew some Y-seams, but it was worth it. It turns out that the birds made the quilt! I also had some leftover hexagons that I used in the border corners. I added the squares in the corners by cutting off the edges of four leftover hexagons and then adding background fabric to make them larger. Refer to Chapter 5: Border Magic (page 34)."*

TRIMMING WONKY STRIPS

LINDA SAYS:

Sometimes, after you have sewn the half-hexagons into strips, you might find some wonky, uneven areas or bulging in the middle of your hexagons. This is usually caused by triangles of slightly different sizes that were created when your ruler slipped as you cut. Or you might have been a little off when sewing the triangles together. Here is how you can fix that.

Use a ruler and rotary cutter to trim the outside edge straight. Don't worry if you cut off some points; it won't matter. Try to keep the width of the strip the same, because it's easy to trim and then have more unevenness on the other side. You also won't have a perfect center match, but in the end you won't notice.

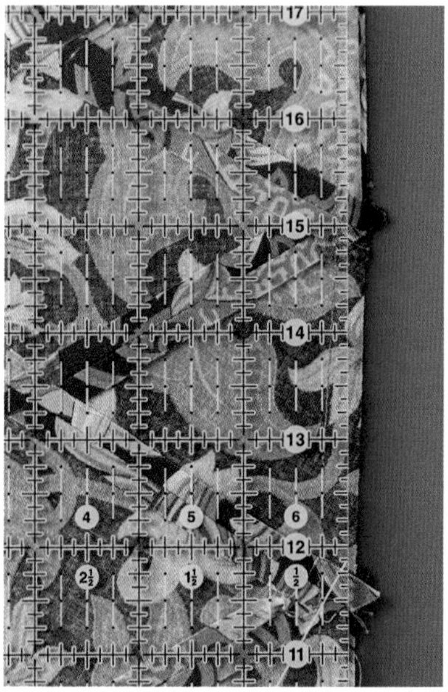

The piecing is off, so the edge of the strip is uneven.

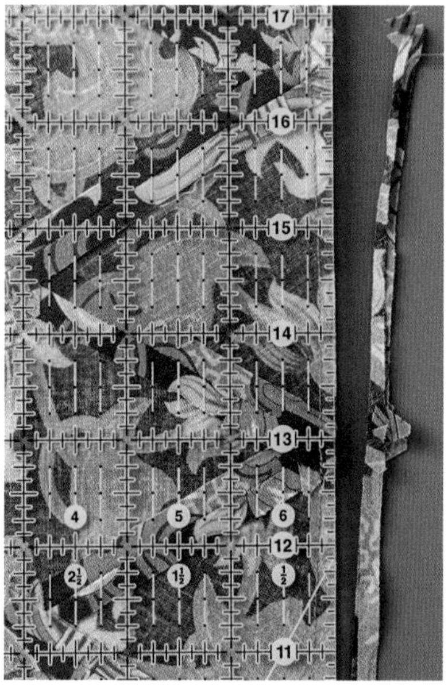

Trim the edge of the strip to even it up.

MAXINE SAYS:

Just press it into submission and quilt the heck out of it.

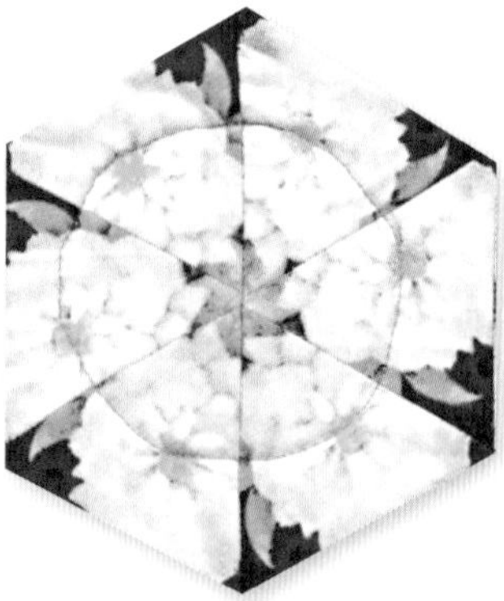

CHAPTER

4

ONE FABRIC, MANY LOOKS

MAXINE SAYS:

I have taught classes in which more than one student started with the same fabric and yet somehow the quilts never looked the same. How could that be? The answer is in how the fabric was cut into strips, what size the triangles were, which color was put into the center of the quilt, how the hexagons were arranged, what the border colors were, and so on.

Every eye sees differently, and so every design will be different. Even if you take all the blocks down and design again in a week, it will be different. As our mood, the temperature, and our attitude changes, so does the design. This is why I always say to let the design sit and to view it in different lighting and on another day.

LINDA SAYS:

When people post an unfinished quilt they are having trouble with, I often ask, "What's the story? What's the title?" There is nothing wrong with a quilt that is just nicely balanced, but I like it when a quilt has a story to tell. That means that there is some intentional design interest. If you're stuck, ask yourself those questions. I've had quilts that stymied me until I found the story (or at least a title).

In the following pages, you will see how different quiltmakers used the same fabric to tell different stories. Here we show you pairs of quilts made from the same fabric but with very different looks. If we had ten quilts for each fabric, each still would be unique and individual.

***My Sunshine Garden*, 35″ × 67″, machine pieced and quilted by May Smith. Pieced using 5″ strips.**

"I found this fabric to be a real challenge because of the many colors in each block. But once I envisioned it as a garden, it came together easily. I echo quilted on each side of the block seams and added curved lines to represent the stamens in the center of each flower. I call this My Happy Quilt."

Detail of *My Sunshine Garden*. Notice how May used her quilting to add stamens to the center of her blocks.

Poppy Explosion, 66″ × 74″, machine pieced and quilted by Liz Granberg, 2015. Pieced using 3¼″ strips.

Original fabric for *My Sunshine Garden* and *Poppy Explosion*: Pandora by Chong-a Hwang for Timeless Treasures. The repeat is 24″.

"I had not intended to make any more OBWs, but when I saw this fabric in a shop close to home, I changed my mind. At another store I found the companion fabrics for the border. I used the feature fabric on the front and added a rich green flange border to separate and emphasize it, so that it looks almost like a panel. To decide on the width of the strips, I measured the repeat and calculated the best width to get the most strips and hexagons for color flow and to leave the least amount of waste. I preferred the smaller units with a more concentrated color that resulted from the nontraditional width."

St. George's Vanquished Dragon, 70″ × 47½″, machine pieced and quilted by Linda Bardes, 2015. Pieced using 4¾″ strips.

"My daughter originally cut the strips but didn't like the hexagons and gave them to me. It was a real struggle to find a layout until I came up with the title, and then the layout just sort of spilled out across my design wall. When I saw the white silk, I knew I had to use that for contrast. Usually I don't like to use the original fabric in my borders, but it worked really well on this quilt next to the small red border that brought out the red in the quilt. I hand quilted horizontally across the hexagons and machine quilted the silk with twelve-gauge white embroidery thread following the lines of the blocks."

Homage to Escher, 44½″ × 40½″, machine pieced and quilted by Maxine Rosenthal. Pieced using 3¼″ strips.

Original fabric for *St. George's Vanquished Dragon* and *Homage to Escher*: Tatsu by Alexander Henry. The repeat is 24″. Both quilters put the fabric on the back of their quilt.

"Cubes can easily be turned into impossible structures, just like Escher did."

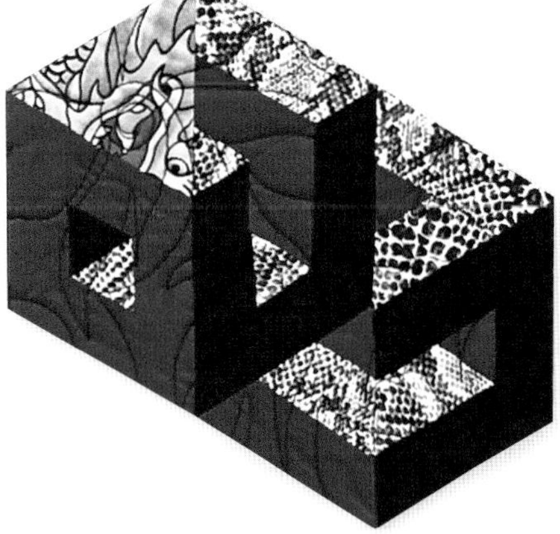

***Reef Hexed*, 56″ × 63¾″, machine pieced and quilted by Kathy Gannon, 2016. Pieced using 3¼″ strips.**

"Both Reef Hexed *and* Under the Sea *were made from cutting only one set of six repeats. When I saw this fabric, I immediately knew I wanted to make a One-Block Wonder with it. I also knew I wanted two smaller wallhangings and not one big quilt. It took some sorting out to make that happen. This was my first time playing with stars, triangles, and blocks."*

Detail of *Reef Hexed*, showing some hexagons close up

Under the Sea; 41¾″ × 43″; machine pieced, appliquéd, and quilted by Kathy Gannon; 2016. Pieced using 3¼″ strips.

Photo by Kathy Gannon

Original fabric for *Reef Hexed* and *Under the Sea*: Tropical Fish by Michael Miller Fabrics

"Notice all the fussy-cut sea life from the original fabric swimming through the quilt."

CHAPTER 5

BORDER MAGIC

HOW BORDERS CHANGE THE DYNAMICS OF A QUILT

Borders are a great way to frame your One-Block Wonder (OBW). After you have assembled the hexagons for your One-Block Wonder, it is a great idea to go shopping to audition fabric for the border. Before the quilt is put together, you only have a vague idea of what will look good as a border.

This is the time to use fabric to point out a color within the quilt body. This works especially well with a narrow inner border (refer to Narrow Inner Borders, page 37).

Many people put the original fabric on the border, but there are other alternatives. Almost every quilt in this book has borders, so you can see a wide variety of ways in which they are used to enhance a finished quilt. We chose a few to highlight in this chapter, including one without any border at all!

MAXINE SAYS:

I want no distraction from the body of the quilt, so I generally use a border fabric similar to the background of the original OBW fabric. I use a lot of fabrics with a black background—black as a border hides so many seams.

Sewing a Triangle into the Border

MAXINE SAYS:

For added interest you can sew a triangle or other shape into the border. Add a wide slice of border fabric around the triangle as though you were making a crazy quilt block, and then cut it to a square or rectangle the same width as the border. Sew it between two strips of border fabric and place it where you want it.

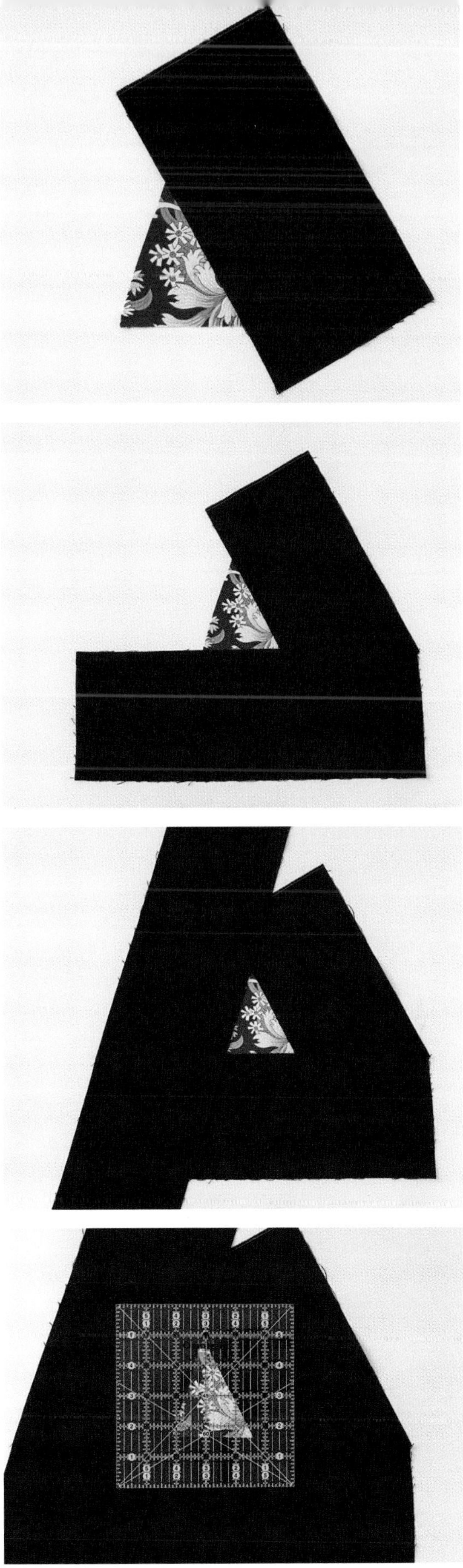

Sew strips of border fabric around a triangle, and cut it into a square the same width as your border.

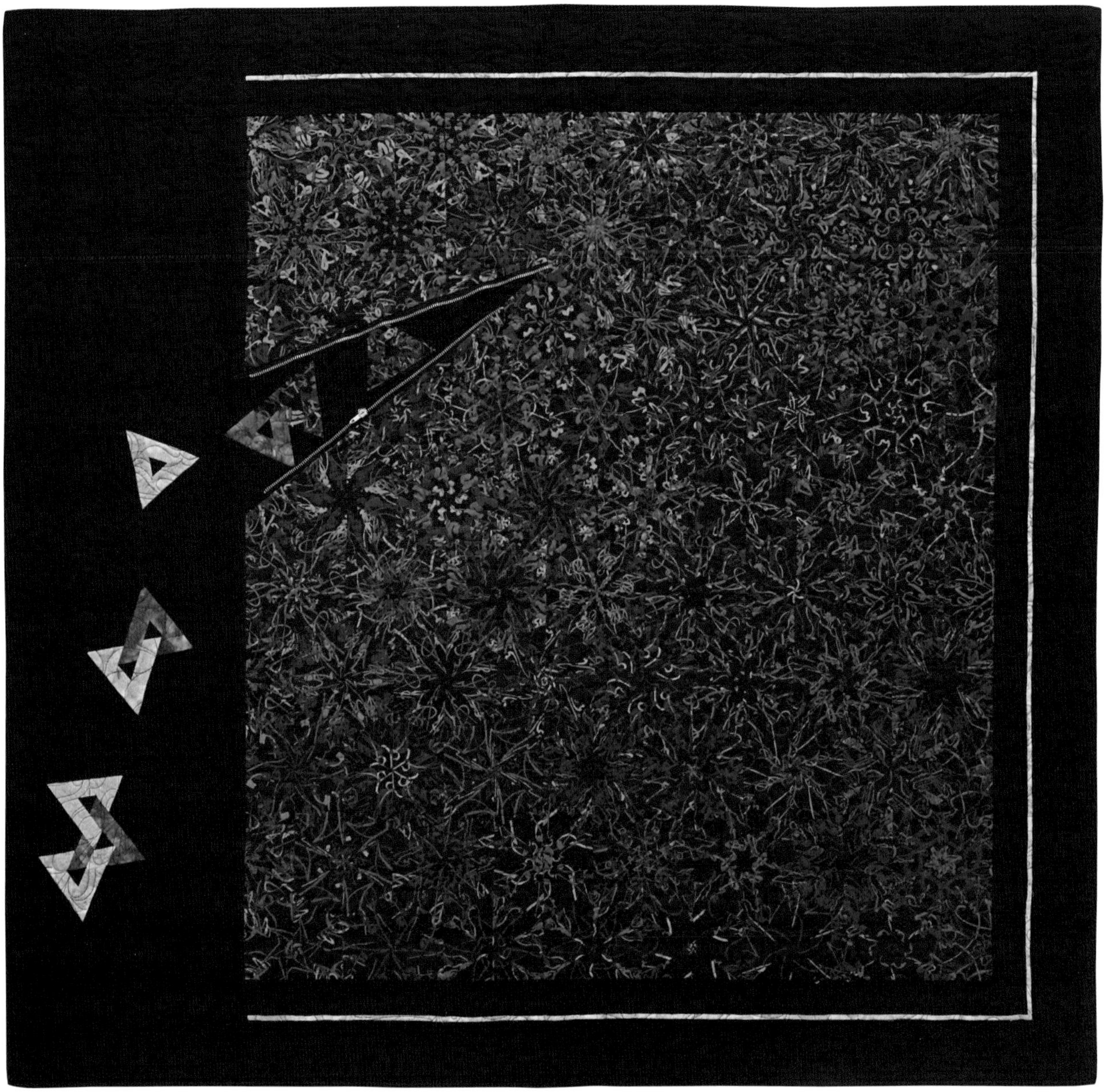

***Unzipped*, 62″ × 60″, machine pieced and quilted by Maxine Rosenthal. Pieced using 3¾″ strips.**

"If you were to unzip a quilt, what would fall out? Here, triangles from the original fabric and the colors within the fabric spill out into the left border. To balance the pop of the green triangles, I added a very narrow inner border of green around the top, right, and bottom sides."

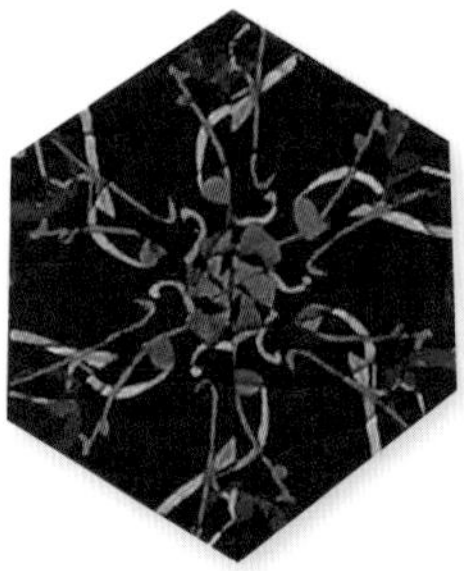

tip

Narrow Inner Borders

There is a great trick for highlighting a specific color within the quilt—a narrow inner border. And by narrow, I mean ¼". It is easy and effective.

1. *Cut a strip ¾" wide.*
2. *Sew this inner border to the quilt as you would normally, and iron the seam allowance toward this wee border.*
3. *Normally we put the next layer to sew on the top, but instead, turn the quilt over with the next border on the bottom. When you are at the machine, you will see the narrow inner border. Usually, since we are concerned with a ¼" seam, we watch the right side of the presser foot so it runs along the edge of the fabric. But if you instead watch the left side of the foot and align it against the last row of stitches, where you added this ¾" strip, you will have a perfect ¼" inner border.*

It doesn't matter if your presser foot is not ¼" on the left side; whatever it is, it will be constant and exact along this entire inner border.

SKETCHING BORDER IDEAS

LINDA SAYS:

I find it helpful to sketch out border ideas, especially if I don't have fabric that will work. I photograph my quilt, print several copies, and paste them onto plain paper. Using colored pencils, I play with colors and different widths for possible borders, and then I check under my bed where I keep my stash. If there is nothing suitable there, I go shopping.

I tried out borders by drawing variations around a quilt photo.

A *Walk in Frida's Garden*, 72″ × 72″, machine pieced and quilted by Jackie O'Brien, 2013. Pieced using 3¾″ strips.

"The fabric and the quilt are based on the art of Frida Kahlo (1907–1954, Mexico). The original fabric forms the left border. The words embroidered in the borders are quotes by Frida. I added cubes to direct the viewer through the garden. This quilt won best in show, first place, and judge's choice in the Mohawk Valley Quilt Club's 2013 show in Whitesboro, New York and second place in the Tidewater Quilters' Guild Virginia's 2014 show in Chesapeake, Virginia."

Detail of *A Walk in Frida's Garden*, showing the original fabric on the left side of the quilt. The original fabric, Frida's Garden by Alexander Henry, has a repeat of 24″.

Frida Kahlo was horribly injured when she was impaled on a piece of metal in a bus accident. She spent a long time in a full-body cast and passed time by learning to paint while lying in bed. Frida often used skulls and butterflies in her paintings. She said that when the cast was removed, she felt like a butterfly escaping its cocoon.

I'm in Paradise, 54¼″ × 63½″, machine pieced and quilted by Betty Berg, 2008. Pieced using 2¾″ strips.

"I purchased ten yards of the fabric because I knew that with the black background, multiple colors, and multiple shapes, I would need to fussy cut the strips and even the triangles to get the right number of colors. I didn't want to use the original fabric in the borders because I thought it would be way too busy. Instead I chose to appliqué some of the flowers using thread painting to highlight the border."

Original fabric for _I'm in Paradise_. The repeat is 22½″.

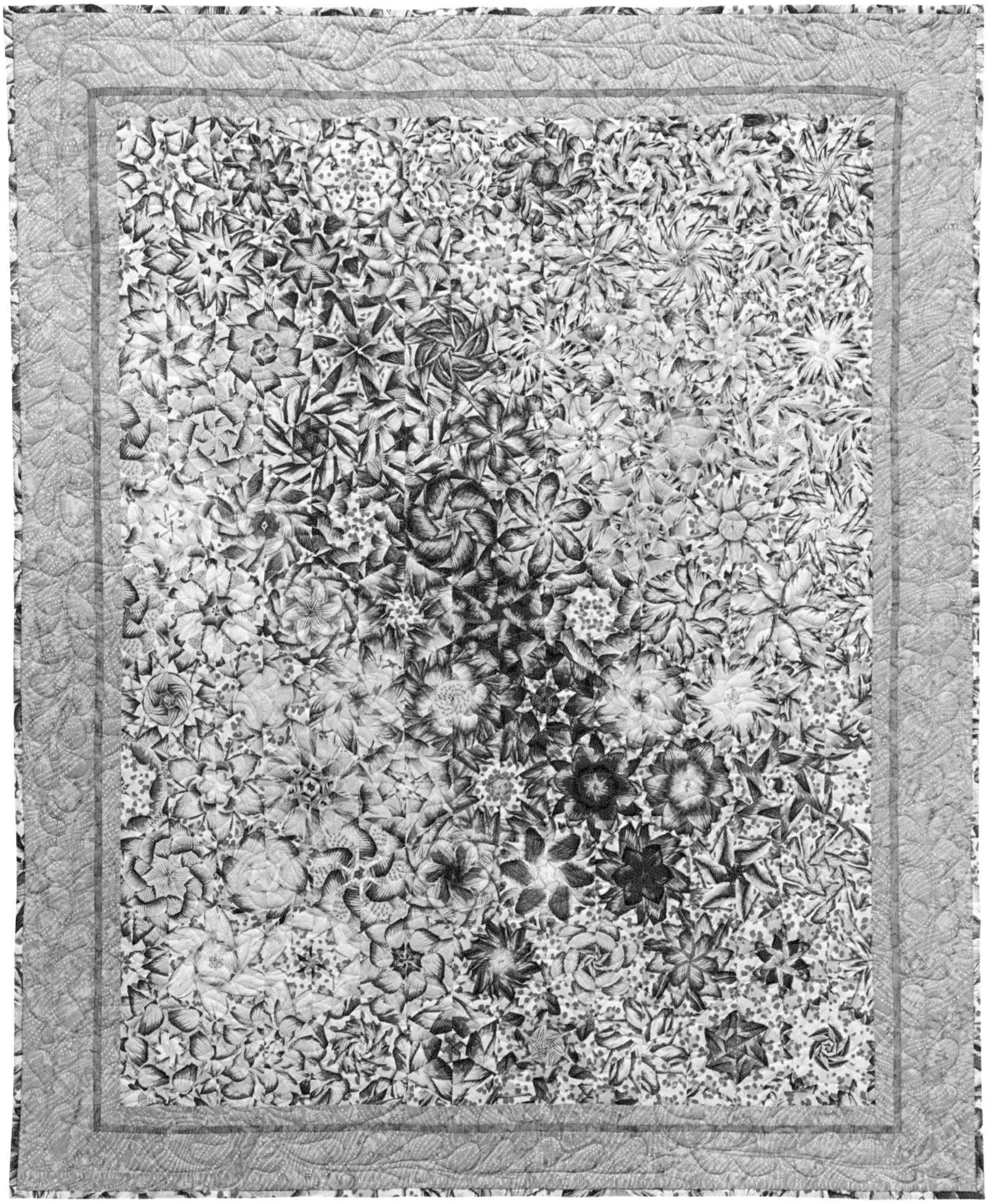

Petals on the Pond, 59″ × 72″, machine pieced by Linda Bardes, machine quilted by Maxine Rosenthal, 2016. Pieced using 3¾″ strips.

Original fabric for *Petals on the Pond*: Leopard Lotus by Philip Jacobs for the Kaffe Fassett Collective (FreeSpirit Fabric). Linda used the fabric on the back of the quilt and in the binding.

"After the struggle with Tropical Sunset *(page 66), I just wanted some pretty fabric that would be easy to design with. My favorite hexagons were the three green ones. I was determined to use them, but it was tricky to keep them from overpowering the design. Even though there is a fair amount of green within the quilt, I needed to bring it out. The narrow green border did that and helped balance everything. I also used the original fabric in the binding. I often do this because I like the way the original fabric on the very outside edge pulls everything together and gives balance to the finished quilt without overpowering it."*

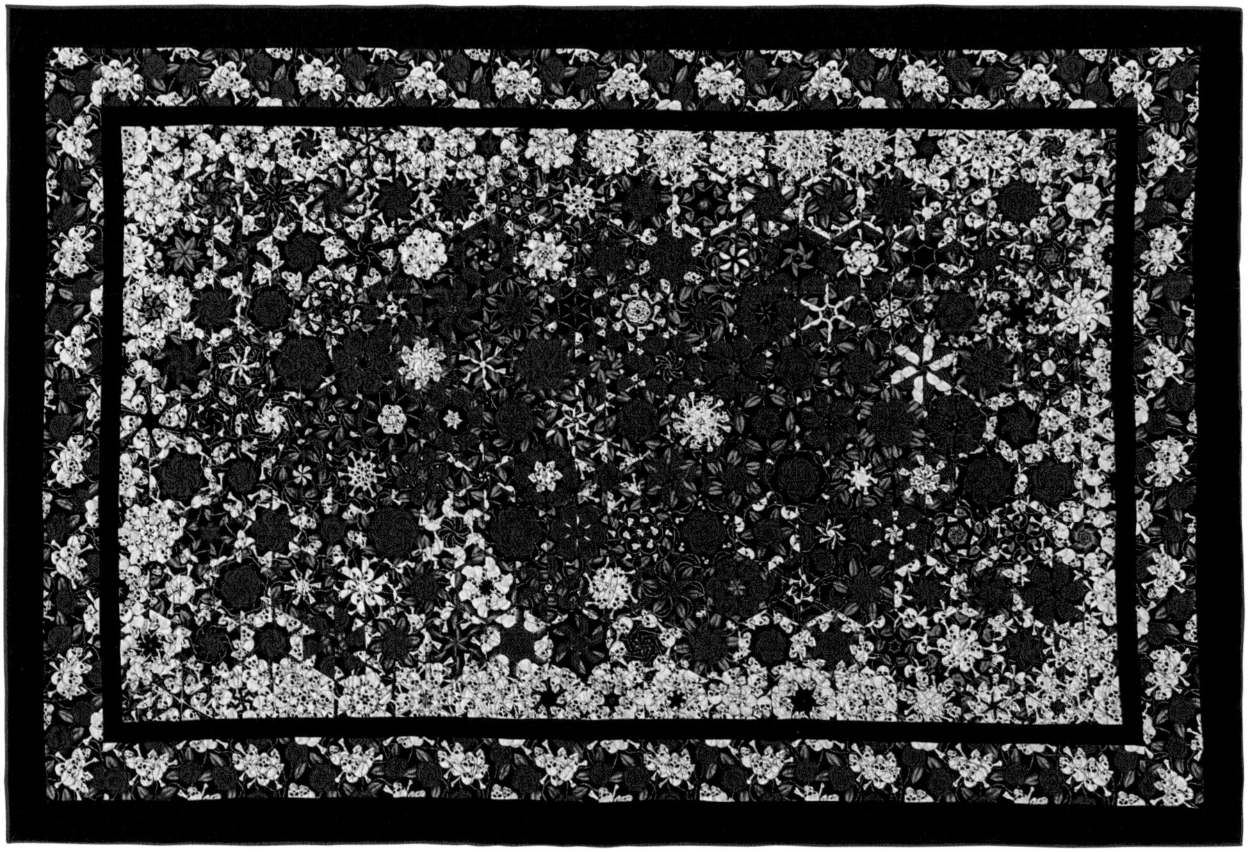

Skulls and Roses, 72″ × 104″, machine pieced and quilted by Linda Williams, 2001. Pieced using 3⅝″ strips.

"I named this quilt Skulls and Roses *because I wanted people to see that something macabre could be made into something beautiful. The design spoke to me right away—I saw a pool of roses surrounded by delicate white flowers. It turned out exactly like I had imagined. Notice how the first border is actually in the main body of hexagons and keeps the outside border from overpowering the design."*

Original fabric in the border of *Skulls and Roses*: Skulls and Roses by Alexander Henry. The repeat is 12″.

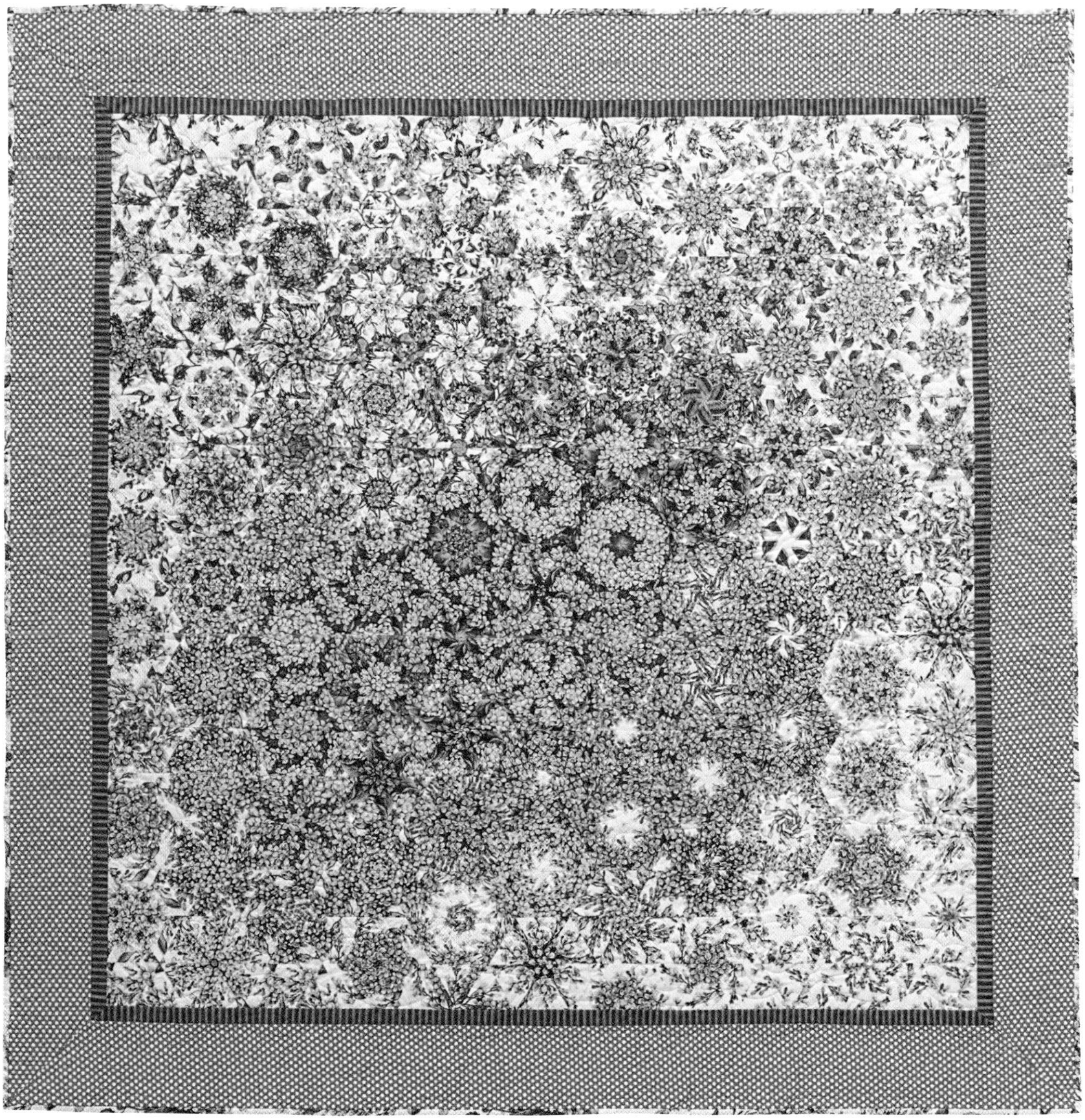

Relay For Life, 68″ × 68″, machine pieced by Jenell Henning, quilted by Lizzie Haskell, 2013. Pieced using 3¾″ strips.

"When my aunt passed away from cancer, I was inspired to make a quilt for Relay For Life. Her favorite color was purple, and the relay also has a purple theme. After I decided on the color, it was hard to locate a fabric that I thought would work. The original fabric had a lot of green that I didn't want, so I pulled out many of the green blocks. Shortly after, a dear quilt friend also passed. I knew then that I needed to add all of my friends' and family's names that have lost this battle. I just recently added my own mother. This quilt, then, is my tribute to them all."

Jumping Jalapeños, 48″ × 49″, machine pieced and quilted by Debbie Peever. Pieced using 3¾″ strips.

"I chose the fabric because of the vibrant jewel tones and decided to cut the strips at the recommended 3¾″ width. I like the flow you get with that size, which breaks up the design in the fabric. I didn't put any borders on this quilt. I auditioned the original fabric, but it just blended in and didn't enhance it. The same with several solid fabrics—they didn't frame the quilt or make it stand out. I decided that the colors were rich enough to stand alone."

Original fabric for *Jumping Jalapeños*: Summer Preserves by Nancy's Cupboard for South Sea Imports

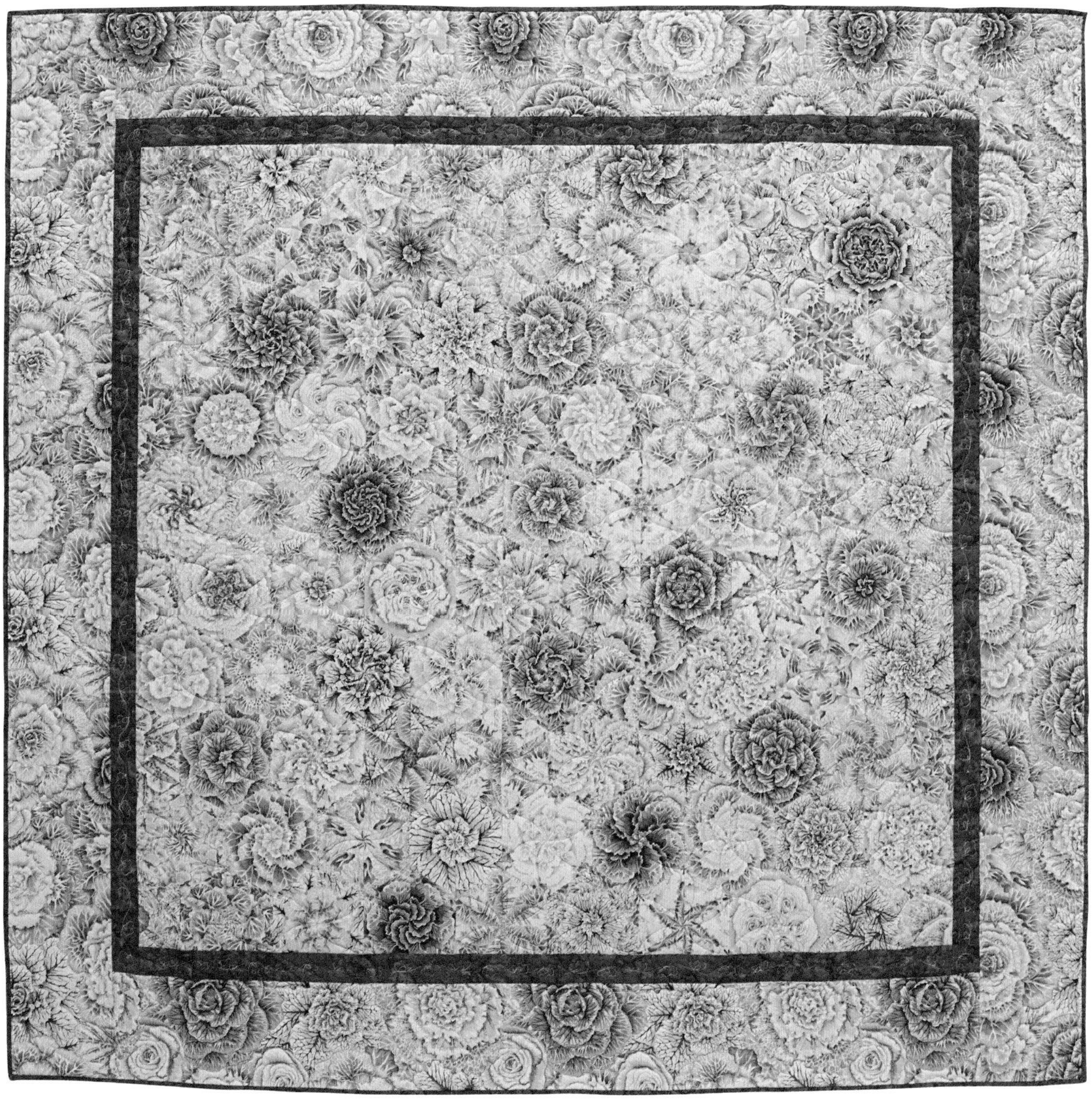

Philip's Green Brassica, 71″ × 69½″, machine pieced and quilted by Lori Johnson, 2015. Pieced using 3¾″ strips.

Original fabric for *Philip's Green Brassica*: Brassica by Philip Jacobs for the Kaffe Fassett Collective (FreeSpirit Fabric). Lori used the original fabric in the outer border and again on the back of the quilt.

"I wanted to make something with fabric from designer Philip Jacobs and chose this fabric for the circular movement in the cabbage roses. After I cut the first four strips, I trimmed off ½″ before cutting again to make sure there were different patterns in the resulting hexagons. The pieced hexagons have a floral look that mimics the original fabric, just more tightly furled because of the piecing. I decided to showcase the original fabric in the border, with a strong purple inner border to separate the pieced hexagons from the original fabric."

Photo by Chris Pearson

***Celestial Dreams*, 70″ × 56″, machine pieced and quilted by Chris Pearson, 2011. Pieced using 3¾″ strips.**

"There is a lot going on in the pattern of this fabric. The majority of the hexagons were bold, and I had trouble finding 'quiet' areas for contrast. I decided to start in the upper left corner with the sun and trail down to the lower right corner with the moons. I left it up on the design wall for weeks—just looking at it, squinting my eyes, and moving the hexagons around to find the best flow of colors. I kept the quilting a simple stitch-in-the-ditch because I didn't want another texture added to this already busy pattern. I used a ½" yellow flange as a color break. Note to self: Don't leave the window open on windy days or turn on the ceiling fan when there is a design wall full of little triangles!"

Photo by Chris Pearson

Original fabric for *Celestial Dreams*: Celestial Dreams by Laurel Burch for Clothworks

CHAPTER 6

BASIC DESIGN HELP

There are some people who design on the floor and others who use a wall. We prefer a design wall. A design wall allows you to see all your blocks from a relatively equal distance. If the blocks are on the floor, some are much farther from you than others, which distorts the layout.

HOW TO ORDER THE BLOCKS BEFORE DESIGNING

MAXINE SAYS:

Begin by dividing your blocks (half-hexagons pinned together) into colors. I look at each block and decide what color it is and then pile others of that color on top of it. When I come upon a block that does not fit that color, I start another pile. I start with the color pile I like the best and place those blocks in the center of the design wall.

The questions you might want to ask at this point include the following:

- Do you want the hexagons in your favorite color to all be in the center, as in a circle, from which other hexagons radiate?
- Do you want these hexagons to be in a diagonal, almost dividing the quilt in half?
- Do you want to start in the center and form a spiral?
- How large will the quilt be?
- Do you want the finished quilt to be a square? A rectangle? A circle?

This is only a starting point. The half-hexagons have been pinned together at this point, so they look whole. This frees you to design and redesign as much as you want. Designing is my favorite part of this whole process. A quilt appears—it begins to tell a story, and I can change that story again and again.

Keep an eye on both the main color of a hexagon and what is going on at its edges. When two or three hexagons are placed together where the outside edges merge into one another—when you can no longer see where one hexagon ends and the next begins—that for me is magic.

LINDA SAYS:

As I pin the half-hexagons together, I set aside the ones I like the best.

After pinning all the hexagons, I use the "smack 'em up" process. I put one or two of those favorites that I have set aside in the center of the design wall, and then I put the remaining blocks on the wall in no particular order. This shows me what I have to work with. It may be that I get an idea for a design at this point, but I don't always.

In any case, I then take the hexagons off the wall and sort them by color, placing each group on a paper plate. Then the designing really begins. Somehow, for me, I simply need to see everything that I have to work with as I begin the project.

hint

One of my mixed-media teachers used to tell us that if we had created a piece of art and didn't know if it was finished or not, to put it on the wall or the floor and keep walking around until it told us what to do. I have had some magical moments with this logic. The same advice works well with a One-Block Wonder—leave the hexagons on the wall, and eventually the design will tell you what to do.

HOW DECONSTRUCTING HEXAGONS CAN HELP

MAXINE SAYS:

Although you have pinned the half-hexagons together, who says they have to stay that way for life? Sometimes half of one hexagon sits so well next to another hexagon, and yet its other half just doesn't fit. Maybe half of another hexagon would look better there.

Whole hexagons

Hexagons made by mixing halves

Although I hate ripping, I am willing to "unsew" for design. I have been known to remove two triangles from half a hexagon and replace them with two triangles from some other hexagon.

It isn't over until the last seam is sewn.

A hexagon made by mixing 4 + 2

In *Midnight in the Garden of Eden* (page 50), many half-hexagons are mixed with different half-hexagons and hexagons with two triangles taken from another hexagon. See how many you can find.

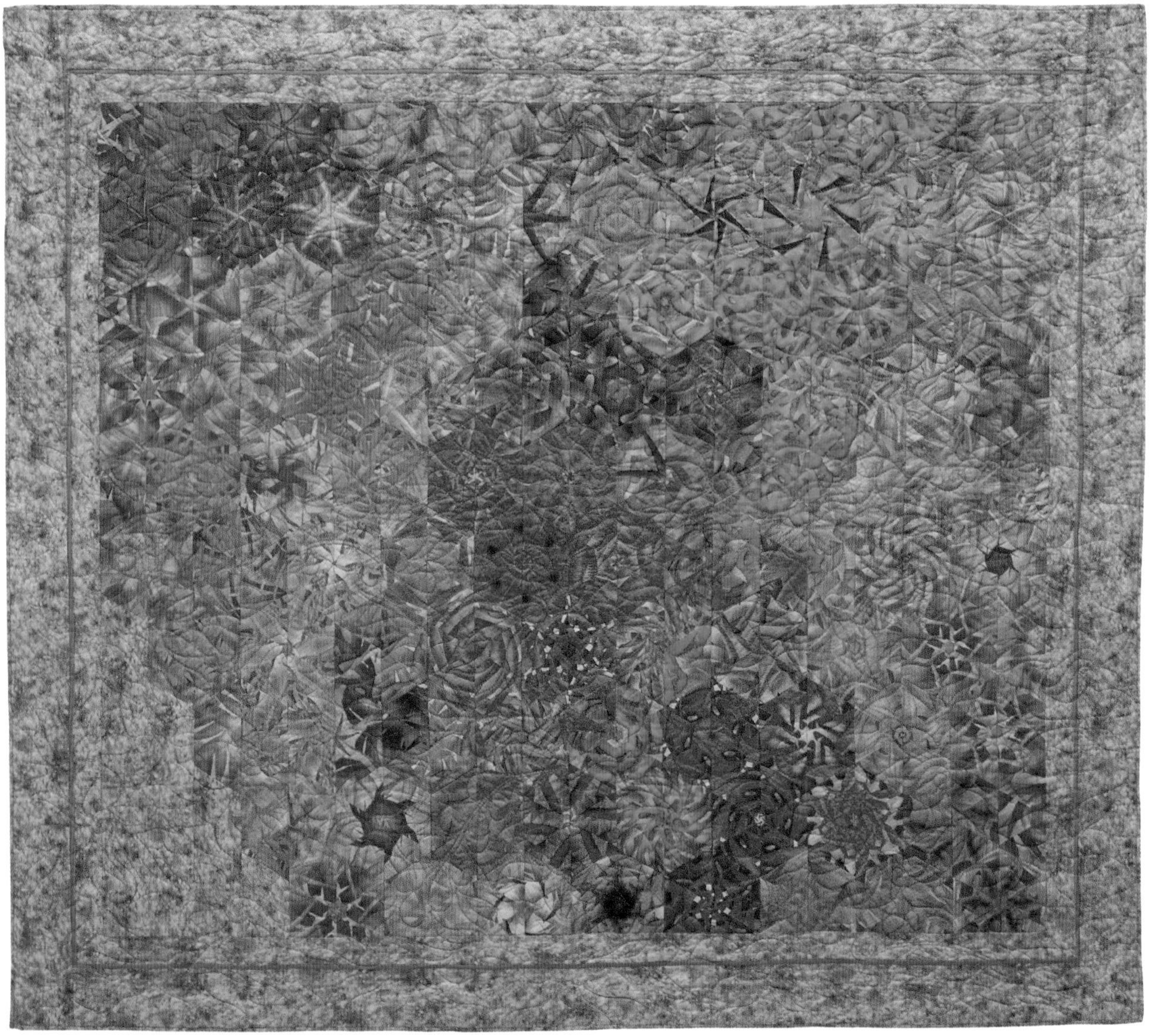

***Midnight in the Garden of Eden*, 66″ × 59″, machine pieced and quilted by Maxine Rosenthal. Pieced using 3¾″ strips.**

"This started with a beautiful fabric with great vibrant colors that I love, but there was hot pink and hot turquoise and yet no half-pink and half-turquoise. So I improvised and told myself a story about a waterfall in the Garden of Eden."

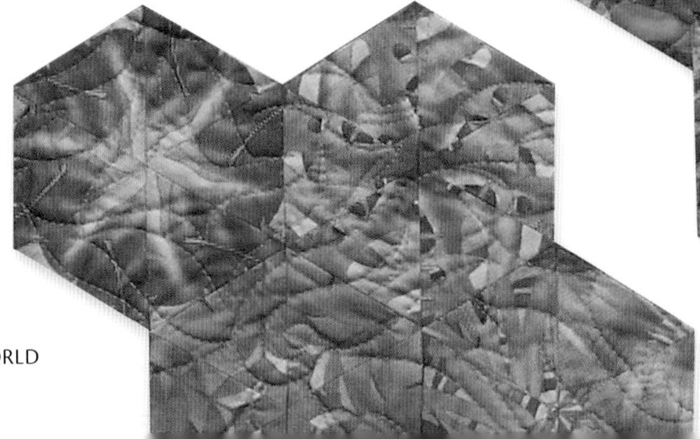

LINDA SAYS:

Sometimes, as you arrange the hexagons, you see an abrupt change in the patterns and flow of the quilt, almost as though there were a line drawn. This can happen if you are using a fabric, such as a panel, that gives you a lot of hexagons that stand alone. In most of our quilts, we are trying to find a flow from one pattern or color to the other. When I find that "line," I can usually get rid of it if I take both halves of a hexagon apart and rearrange the triangles. What was on the inside might work if it is turned to the outside edge.

MAKING YOUR DESIGN PORTABLE

LINDA SAYS:

My design work with *Tropical Sunset* (page 66) was interrupted by a five-week trip to Arizona. I wanted to keep working with the story for the quilt, which was very hard to arrive at, so I came up with this portable design idea: I took a picture of all the hexagons on the design wall and printed it out as large as I could. Then I cut out all of the hexagons and put them in an envelope. When I wanted to work with them, I simply found a foundation to lay them on and kept designing. It was a struggle, but finally my daughter came up with the perfect layout! I was very excited, but when our backs were turned, her furry friends took over. Although I could not reproduce the exact design from "before the cats," I had the basic idea in mind. I was able to build on that to arrive at a design I thought worked really well.

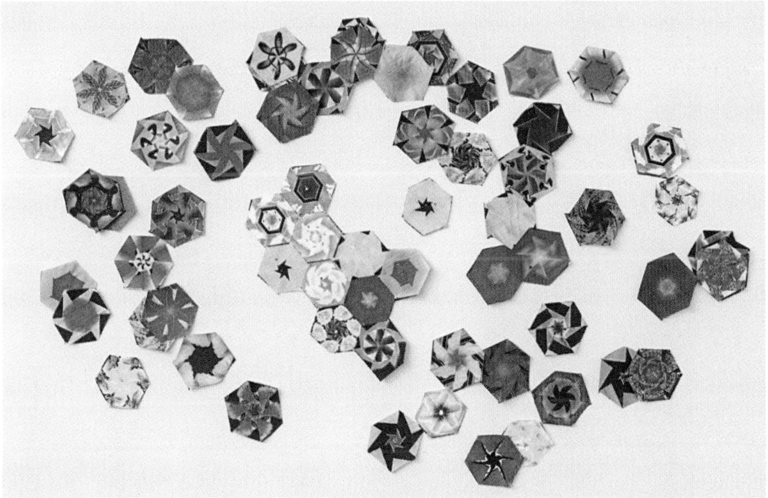

Mini hexagons on a mat

Design board malfunction

The start of a new layout

THE WONDER ROSE—A 3D DESIGN ELEMENT FOR LEFTOVERS

MAXINE SAYS:

My friend Nancy Miller has come up with a most inventive idea for extra or not-so-extra blocks. First she sews a hexagon together and presses it. Then she cuts a muslin hexagon base smaller than that hexagon. She pins the larger hexagon to the muslin base at each corner. Because it is larger, she makes small folds to make it fit to the muslin base. Do this on all six sides, with the fold in the same direction, and then sew the outside edge to the base within the seamline. There will be a puff or mountain in the center. Give that a twist, and tack down the center with a few hand stitches.

The resulting hexagons are a little smaller than the flat hexagons, but you can easily fit them in the corners of the border or along one edge of the border.

Two Wonder Roses sewn together. The three-dimensional twist at the center highlights the repeated elements in the hexagon.

LINDA SAYS:

This new technique stretches the basic One-Block Wonder process designed by Maxine in new and creative dimensions. If you want to use a Wonder Rose in the body of a quilt, you must plan ahead so that one of the strips is cut at least ¾″ to 1″ wider (or more) than all the other hexagons. Cut a muslin hexagon or use any left-over hexagon that is the same size as a finished hexagon in your quilt. (You will have to sew one together to find the size.) Sew the six triangles together. Lay the larger hexagon on the muslin and pin the corners. Then follow the instructions at left. If you incorporate the Wonder Rose within the quilt, expect to make some Y-seams.

Here you see the larger hexagon positioned over the smaller one. Line up the points and pin. To take the fullness off the outside edges, make a tuck and pin it so it lies flat against the hexagon underneath. Sew the two edges together ⅛″ from the edge. Now twist or spin the middle to get it to "flower." The bigger the difference between the two hexagons, the more fabric you will have to twist to create the rose. You will notice that the twin example (at left) has a tighter center. It was at least an inch larger than the base. The one you see here is a little looser because the top was ¾″ bigger. Add a button or bead in the middle or simply stitch it down to hold it in place.

CHAPTER

7

DESIGN OPPORTUNITIES

In the quilts that follow, the quiltmakers used various design styles to show their hexagons off to the best advantage. Here's hoping you find inspiration in their work!

DIAGONAL DESIGN

When you arrange the colors of the hexagons in a diagonal pattern, it can look as if a ray of light is spilling through your quilt.

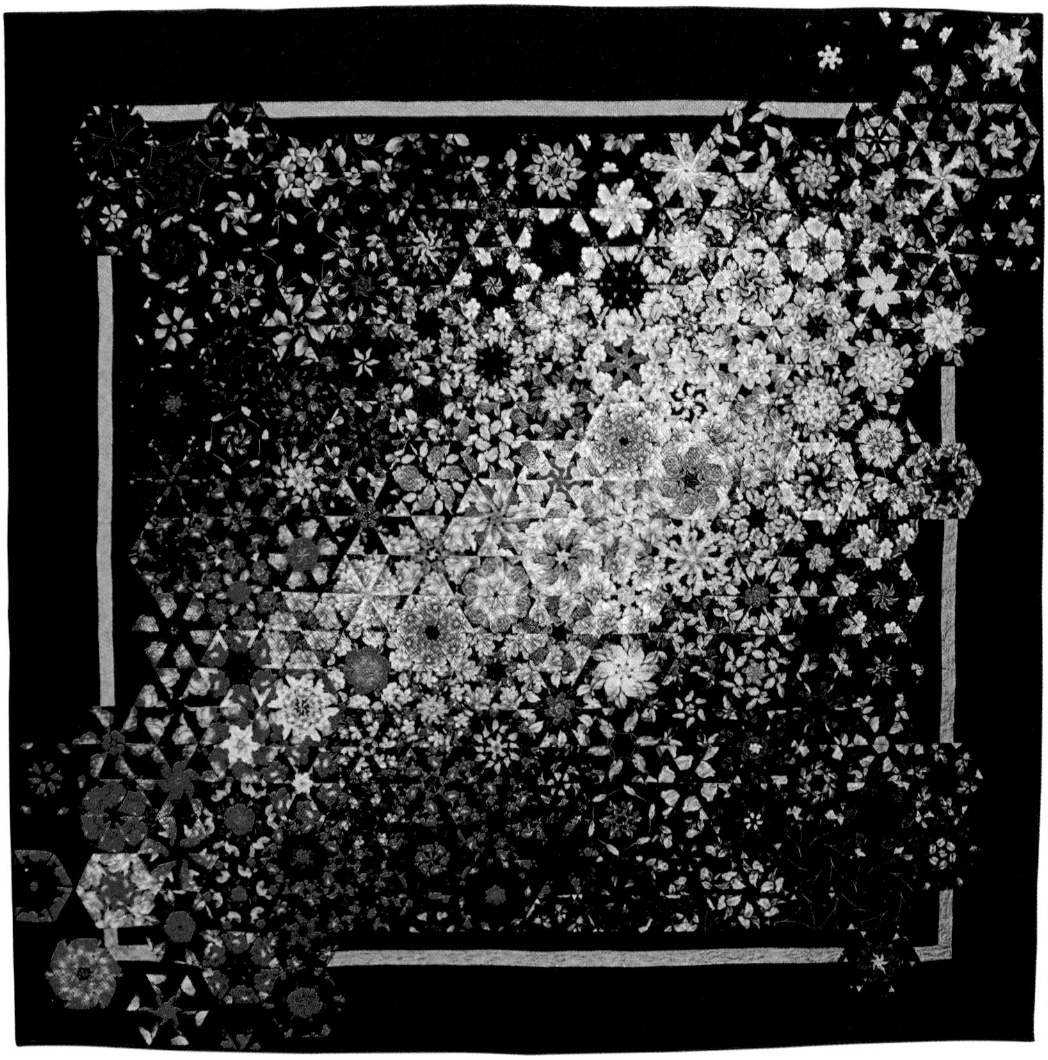

Photo by Ed Arnold of Capturing Life Photography

***Galactic Gardens*, 77″ × 79″, designed by Emma Hufman,**
machine pieced and quilted by Karen Hufman, 2016. Pieced using 3¾″ strips.

"Each of my grandchildren receives a quilt of his or her choosing when they graduate from high school and college, and one when they get married. Emma graduated high school in 2016, and she designed this. Here are her words: 'Since I am a very indecisive person, the idea of using only one fabric really appealed to me. Grandma and I went out on the annual quilt hop, and I became doubtful that I would ever find the fabric I wanted. The very last store had exactly the right fabric. I couldn't be happier with the way it turned out and the time I was able to spend working on it with my grandma.' This quilt won a first place and best of show at the 2016 Kansas State Fair."

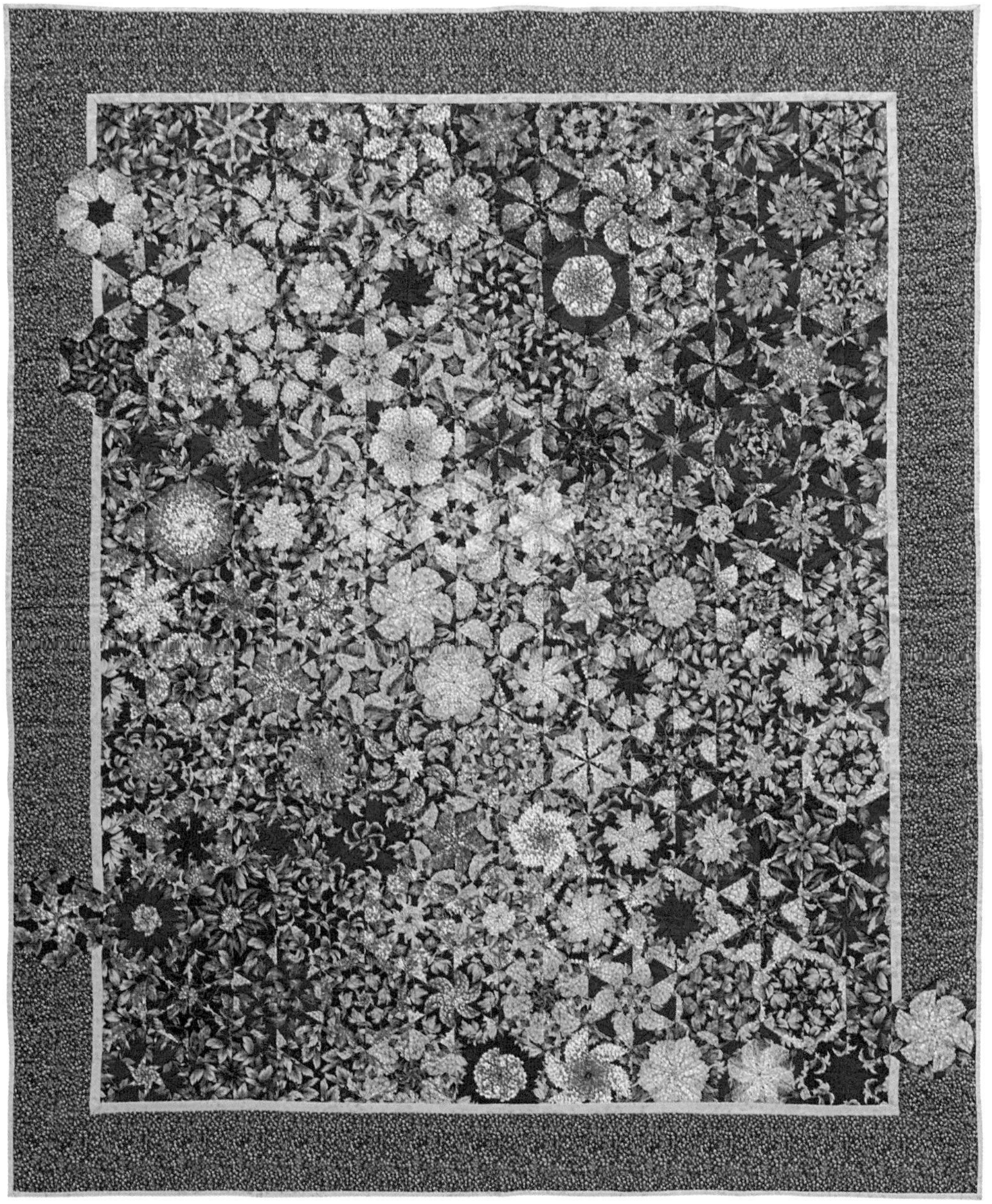

Ray of Light, 77″ × 79″, machine pieced and quilted by Joan Kruse, 2014. Pieced using 3½″ strips.

"I found the fabric on clearance in an online shop. The yellow and blue hydrangeas on the dark background were calling my name. I chose the fabric because it had the perfect colors for my brother and sister-in-law's house. This is my first OBW."

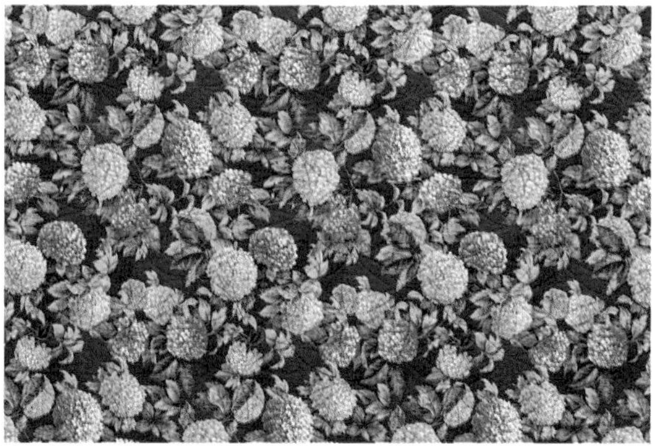

Original fabric for *Ray of Light*: Summer Breeze III by Sentimental Studios for Moda Fabrics. Joan added the fabric to the back of the quilt.

SWIRLS

Arranging the colors in a swirl creates a lot of movement in the quilt.

***Partridge in a Pear Tree*, 84″ × 94″, machine pieced and quilted by Sue Sharpe. Pieced using 3¾″ strips.**

"I purchased enough fabric for twelve repeats. The first six repeats were from the original yardage, and then I removed 2″ of fabric before the next set so the repeats would be slightly different. I chose the fabric because I loved everything about it. While sewing, I placed a couple of pinecones in one of the cubes and fused a partridge on top of another one."

Original fabric for *Partridge in a Pear Tree*

Photo by Malcom Whitfield

Eye of the Storm, 76″ × 86″, machine pieced and quilted by Barb Frost, 2015. Pieced using 3¾″ strips.

Original fabric for *Eye of the Storm*. The repeat is approximately 12″.

"I made several Stack-n-Whacks before I saw my first One-Block Wonder. I found a fabric design that was big and bulky and that I would never otherwise take home. Once I had measured, pinned, cut strips, and then cut triangles—all according to instructions—I thought, 'What in the world am I doing? Is this fun?' But I slogged along until all the half-hexagons were pinned together. Then it began to get exciting. I put them up on the wall and rearranged them a few times; then I took them all down and started again with a definite plan. Ta-da! I was done! And yes, it was fun."

CUBES

If you have chosen a fabric that has only a few colors, such as blue and white, you will have an abundance of hexagons with only those few colors. You may want to add other elements to create interest. In these quilts, the designers show you how adding cubes or blocks takes a bland color scheme and transforms it.

hint

When you place cubes in your layout, keep in mind that a virtual light will be shining from the top to the bottom or from the top edges diagonally down through the cubes. Arrange your cube fabrics so that the "shadows" are at the bottoms of the cubes and the lighter sides are facing toward the top of the quilt.

Photo by Tim Barnwell

***Sterling Block Party*, 44″ × 39″, machine pieced and quilted by Jean Condon. Pieced using 3½″ strips.**

"This panel contains my favorite color combinations. I wanted to make the big hollow cube featured in the quilt Block Party *from* One-Block Wonders Cubed! *(by C&T Publishing). During the design process, I decided to set aside some of the hexagons with the bold yellow lines because these detracted from the large hollow cube I was making. I saved them for another quilt. I found this panel challenging to design with, and the large hollow cube added another challenge. Perseverance = big win!"*

Photo by Tim Barnwell

Detail of *Sterling Block Party*

Photo by Tim Barnwell

Original fabric for *Sterling Block Party*: Star of Hope by Benartex, a 21″ × 40″ panel

Photo by Ada Bahlman

***Winter at the Farm*, 58″ × 51″, machine pieced by Els Helleman, quilted by Elly Prins, 2016. Pieced using 3¾″ strips.**

"While visiting a friend in Canada, I visited an Amish lady's house and fell in love with this fabric showing horses in the snow. Eventually I found some to buy. When I finished the layout, it seemed very bland. So I decided to add the cubes for more color. The longarm quilter quilted an overall pattern of snowflake crystals."

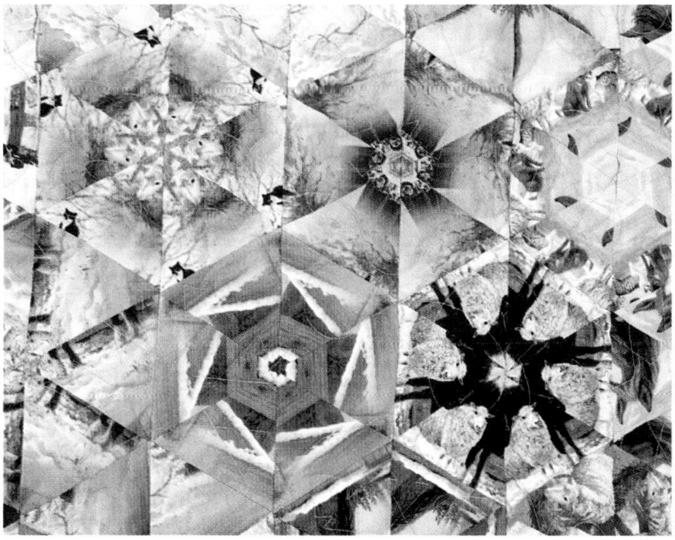

Photo by Ada Bahlman

Detail of *Winter at the Farm*, showing a close-up of the hexagons. The horses disappear, and snow crystals appear instead.

Photo by Ada Bahlman

Original fabric for *Winter at the Farm*

Iowa Cows, 67″ × 40″, machine pieced and quilted by Cynthia Bosley. Pieced using 3¾″ strips.

"As I worked with the fabric, I couldn't help but think of a blackjack or baccarat table, and so I began to incorporate cubes to help work against those associations. The quilt brought me a certain amount of tongue-in-cheek smirking, since I'd grown up in town where the meatpacking plants were prominent and my own cutting and piecing was far less fragrant!"

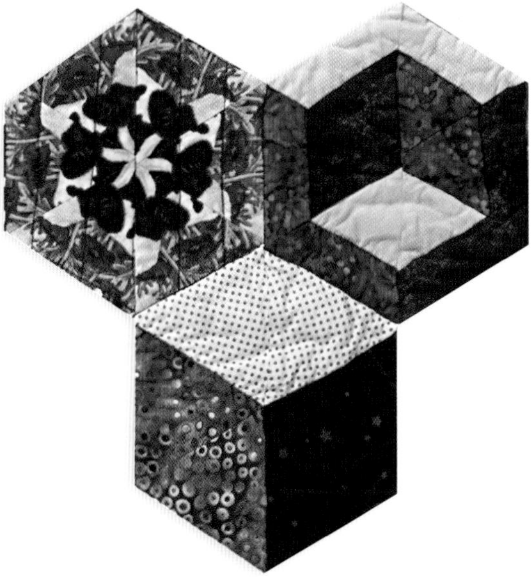

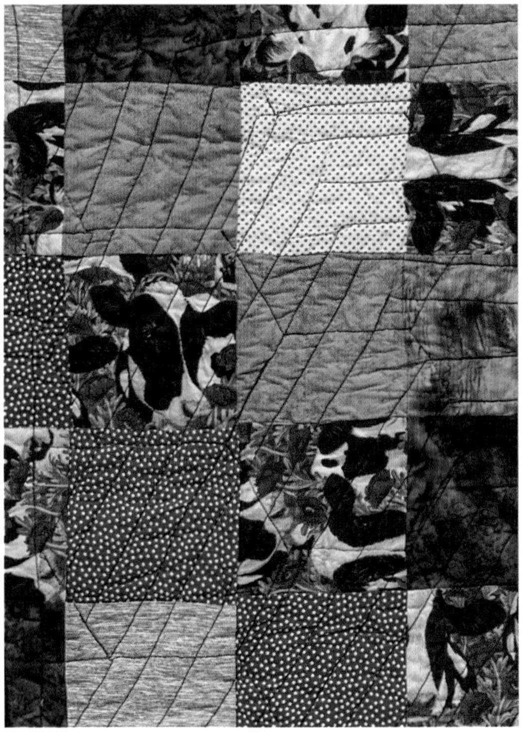

Original fabric for *Iowa Cows*: Cows and Poppies by Patty Reed Designs for Fabric Traditions. The repeat is approximately 12″. Cynthia used the fabric on the back of the quilt.

ADDING INTEREST

These quilters spiced up their quilts with appliqué elements from the original fabrics.

Photo by Tim Barnwell

Fun in the Jungle, 71″ × 90″, machine pieced and quilted by Jean Condon. Pieced using 3½″ strips.

Photo by Tim Barnwell

Detail of *Fun in the Jungle*

Photo by Tim Barnwell

Original fabric for *Fun in the Jungle*: Jomo Jungle Border by Alexander Henry. The repeat is 22½″. Jean Condon used the original fabric within the quilt. (You have to look a bit to find it!)

"The soft colors and shapes were what first attracted me to the fabric. At first I wasn't excited about the animals and had no problem cutting them up. Yet the more I worked with them, the more enamored I became of them. I decided to incorporate the piece I had saved for the back into the front. I added large borders to make room to appliqué the monkey and toucan to frame the design."

Photo by Leslie Davidson

***Nana's Flower Garden*, 61½″ × 86½″, machine pieced and quilted by Diana Eaton, 1997. Pieced using 3½″ strips.**

Photo by Leslie Davidson

Diana used the original fabric in the top border of *Nana's Flower Garden*.

"This quilt is my first One-Block Wonder. I was attracted by the dragonflies in the fabric and hoped it would be suitable. However, almost half the completed hexagons were very similar, so it was difficult to arrange them in the allover layout described in One-Block Wonders*. I decided on a more traditional arrangement, and Grandmother's Flower Garden seemed to work best. It was also appropriate since I was making the quilt for my mother-in-law, a grandmother of eleven."*

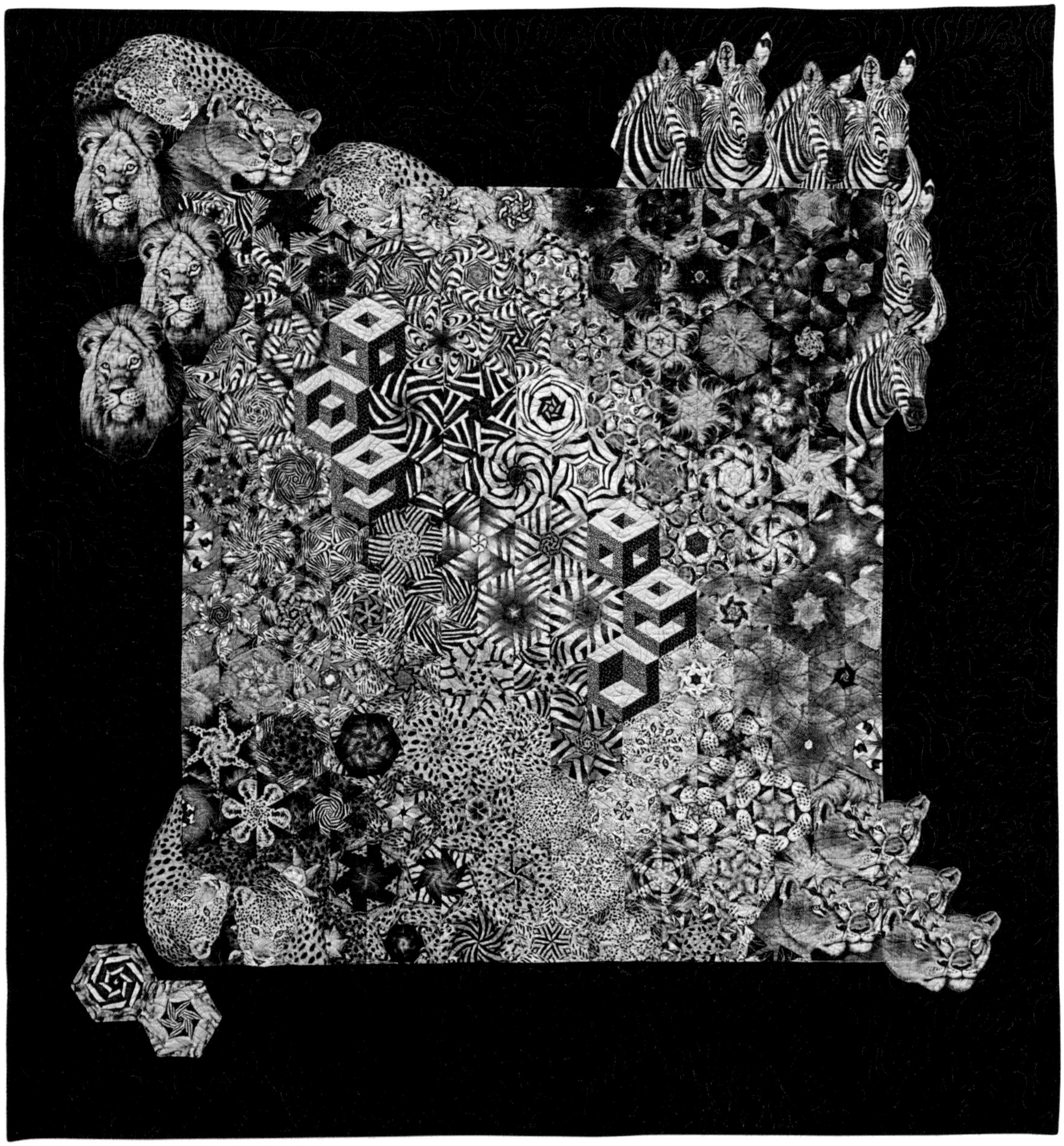

Just Lion Around, 84″ × 88″, machine pieced and quilted by Jackie O'Brien, 2008. Pieced using 3¾″ strips.

Original fabric for *Just Lion Around*: Lion Eyes by Alexander Henry. The repeat is 24″. Jackie used the fabric on the quilt back.

"I fell in love with the fabric and just had to make an OBW out of it. At the border corners, I appliquéd the animals to pop out of the pieced blocks."

Photo by Bart Huscher of About Faces Photography

Follow the Light, 58½″ × 60″, machine pieced and quilted by Sue Fenwick. Pieced using 3¾″ strips.

"I learned how to do a One-Block Wonder from Maggie Hamilton at a retreat in California. Then I decided to try adding some hollow cubes. I found fabric that closely matched the palette in the main fabric, but I made the cubes thinner because I wanted them to appear lighter. Then I posted photos on the Facebook group, where Korinna Schwerd worked with me on focusing where I was orienting the source of light in the design. The logical and spiritual choice is the upper right. I arranged the hexagons so that the light flowed from dark in the lower left up to light in the upper right corner. I think the result is that the cubes appear to float up to the light, and the light in the upper right corner illuminates the cubes."

Original fabric for *Follow the Light*: Feathers by Philip Jacob for the Kaffe Fassett Collective (FreeSpirit Fabric). The repeat is 24″.

Photo by René Hermans

Aves Volantes*, 37″ × 53″, machine pieced and quilted by Helena Kieser, 2015. Pieced using 3¾″ strips.

"The name is Latin for 'Birds in Flight.' I wanted to attempt an OBW but didn't want to buy any fabric. Fortunately, this fabric was in my stash. When I finished sewing the strips together, I cut the bottom of the strips straight but left the top zigzag. Then I added an appliqué strip with the birds over the top edge."

Photo by René Hermans

Detail of *Aves Volantes*

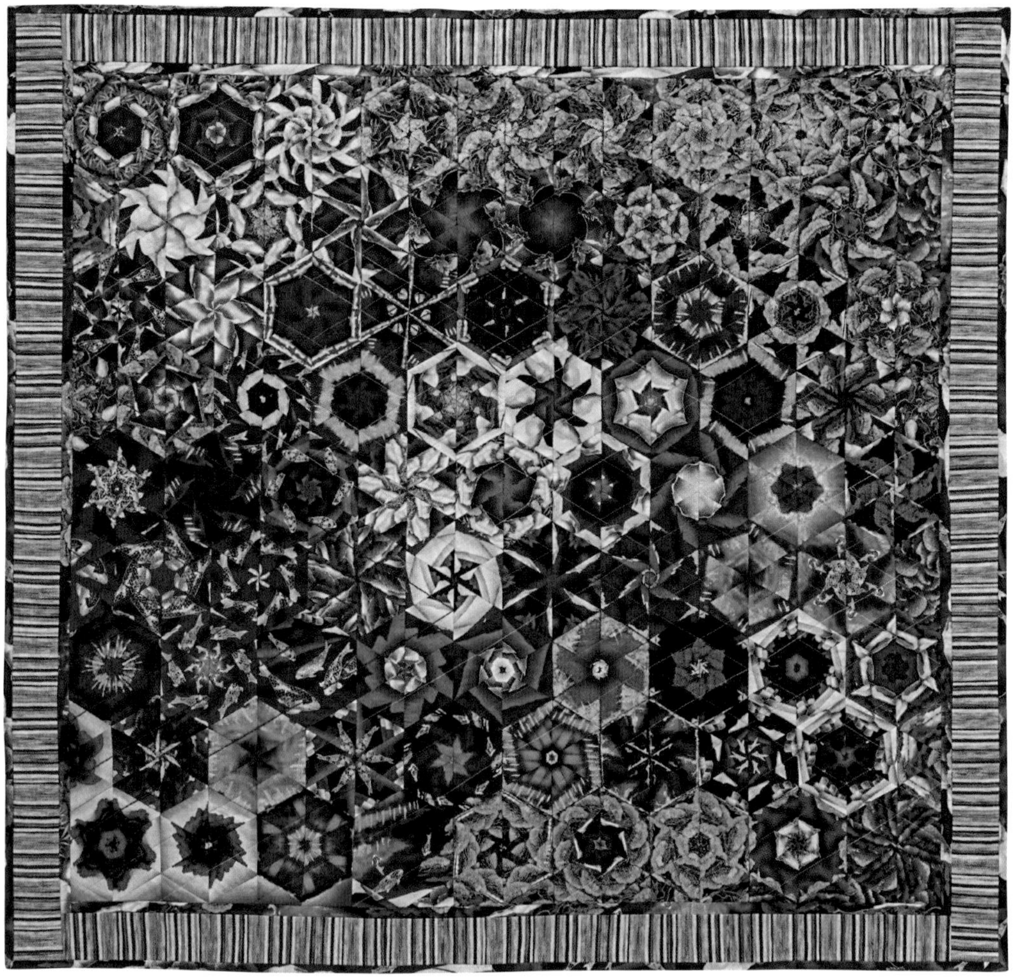

***Creation*, 51″ × 55″, machine pieced and quilted by Linda Bardes, 2013. Pieced using 3¾″ strips.**

"This was the first fabric I bought to make a One-Block Wonder, but my second quilt. I was seduced by the colors and the pattern and had a lot of trouble getting a design I liked. There were a lot of leftover hexagons. I named it Creation *because of the fish in the design, which brought to mind the Bible passage that goes something like, 'First God created the heavens, then the seas and the fishes, and out of the waters came every living thing.' There were three blocks that jumped right off the quilt, yet they had so much interest that I wanted to use them. To make it work, I used some gold enamel that matched the gold in the fabric and painted in some hexagons to bring balance to the design."*

Detail of *Creation*, showing some gold painting on the hexagons

Linda used this Japanese print, the original fabric for *Creation*, on the back of the quilt. The repeat is 24″.

PREPRINTED PANELS

Remember Using Panels (page 13), in Chapter 2, where we said that designing with panels is a challenge? These quilters met the challenge beautifully! For more beautiful quilts made with panels, see *Sterling Block Party* (page 58) and *Tropical Sunset* (page 66).

***Girl Dreaming of Kaleidoscopes and Tumbling Blocks*, 49″ × 40″, machine pieced and quilted by Sharon Moos, 2015. Pieced using 3¾″ strips.**

"I fell in love with this panel and bought nine of them. After I cut the strips and assembled the half-hexagons, I had no idea how to proceed. I knew I wanted the girl to be seen. At first I tried placing half-hexagons around the panel, but that wasn't working. Then I hung one of the panels on my design wall and used it to help me fussy cut a few whole hexagons. When the quilt was finished, it looked like I had incorporated part of an entire panel when actually those parts are made up of whole hexagons."

Original fabric for *Girl Dreaming of Kaleidoscopes and Tumbling Blocks*: Princess on a Pea around the World—Prairie panel by Denyse Klette for Elizabeth's Studio. Sharon used the panel on the back of the quilt. On the front of the quilt, she stitched in-the-ditch to create a simple diamond pattern, which makes a beautiful design on the back of the quilt.

Tropical Sunset, 61″ × 84″, machine pieced and quilted by Linda Bardes, 2016. Pieced using 4¼″ strips.

"First I fell in love with this panel. It was so unlike anything I had seen used as an OBW that I was determined to step into the mystery and see what would reveal itself. I played with strips of paper and cut-out triangles to try and get a sense of how wide to cut the strips. I ended up with 4¼″ because I didn't want too many red and yellow-orange hexagons, which were the main colors. I was looking for drama, and I certainly got what I wanted. Adding the four small panels to the side only added to the story."

Original fabric for *Tropical Sunset*: Twelve Moons by Sybil Shane for Robert Kaufman Fabrics. The repeat is 24″. Linda put the panel on the back of the quilt.

Original fabric for *Wanderlust: Paris in Spring*: a Hoffman Spectrum Digital screen print. The repeat is 17″.

Wanderlust: Paris in Spring, 45″ × 59″, machine pieced and quilted by Liz Granberg (Gypsy Dreamer Quilts), 2015. Pieced using 3¼″ strips.

"I was not new to the OBW process. But I was reinspired by the Facebook group to think about using panels instead of allover prints. I decided I wanted to feature the panel on the front and incorporate it within the color flow. I decided to cut the strips slightly smaller than usual because I wanted more hexagons to play with. As a final touch, I added a three-dimensional ¼″ flange border of a contrasting color around the panel to set it off from the color flow. My interest in turning panels into hexified panel quilts—my twist on the original OBW—has reignited my work. I have twelve quilts at this writing, and many more panels waiting in my sewing room."

NOVELTY DESIGNS

These quilters took their artwork a step further and created secondary designs with the color placement of the hexagons.

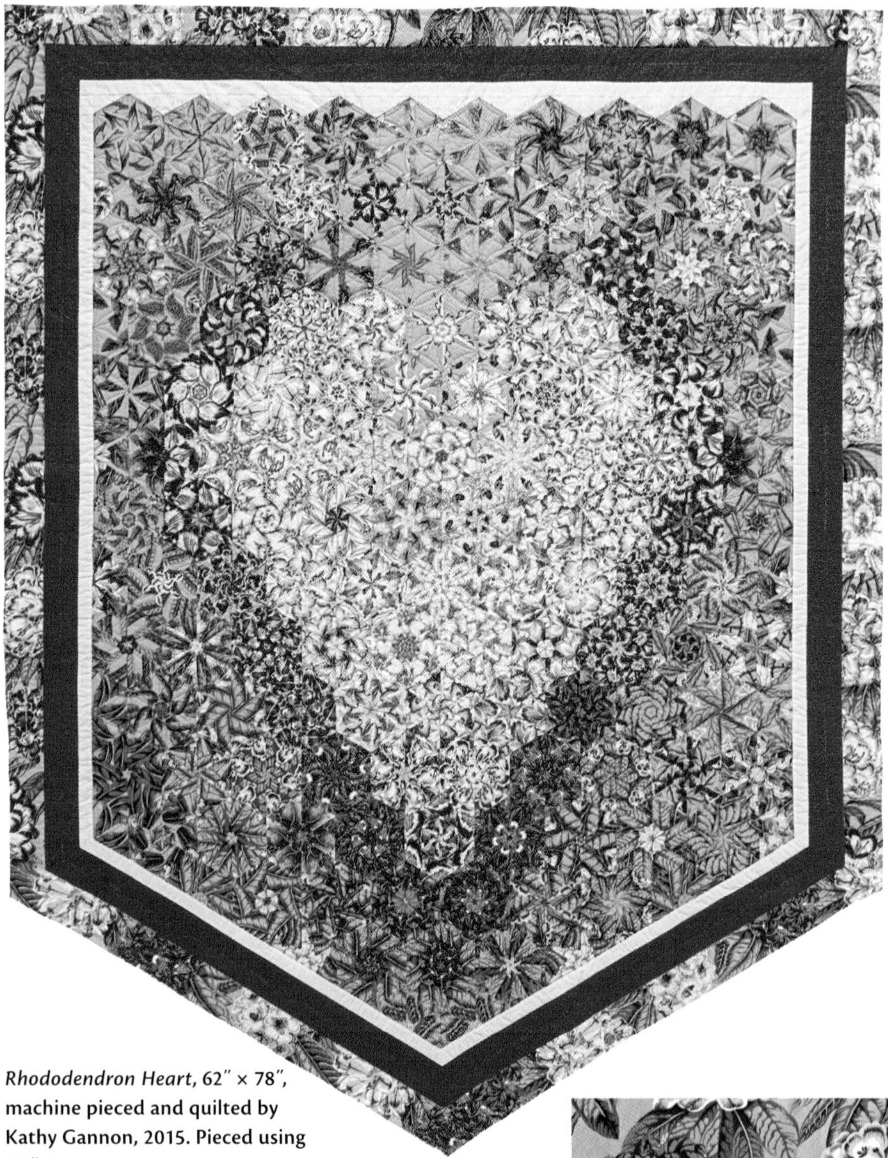

***Rhododendron Heart*, 62″ × 78″, machine pieced and quilted by Kathy Gannon, 2015. Pieced using 3¼″ strips.**

"I chose this fabric for the colors and my love of flowers. This design evolved slowly after trying several different layouts. I learned that sometimes the fabric has more to say on the outcome than we do! And one fabric really can yield very different results."

Photo by Kathy Gannon

Original fabric for *Rhododendron Heart*: Rhodondrons by Snow Leopard Designs for FreeSpirit Fabric. The repeat is 23½″.

***Comfort and Joy*, 94″ × 105″, machine pieced by Verlie Murphy, machine quilted by Elaine Hewitt. Pieced using 1¼″ strips.**

"This quilt was a commission from my friend Frances Fairey. She gave me free rein to make it as artistic as I chose. Until I discovered Maxine's books, I had only made a few quilts. I took her basic ideas and went a little wild with them, playing with cubes, and now I am addicted. The title came to me from the fact that it was to be used on her bed—comfort—and 'joy' because it speaks volumes of love throughout."

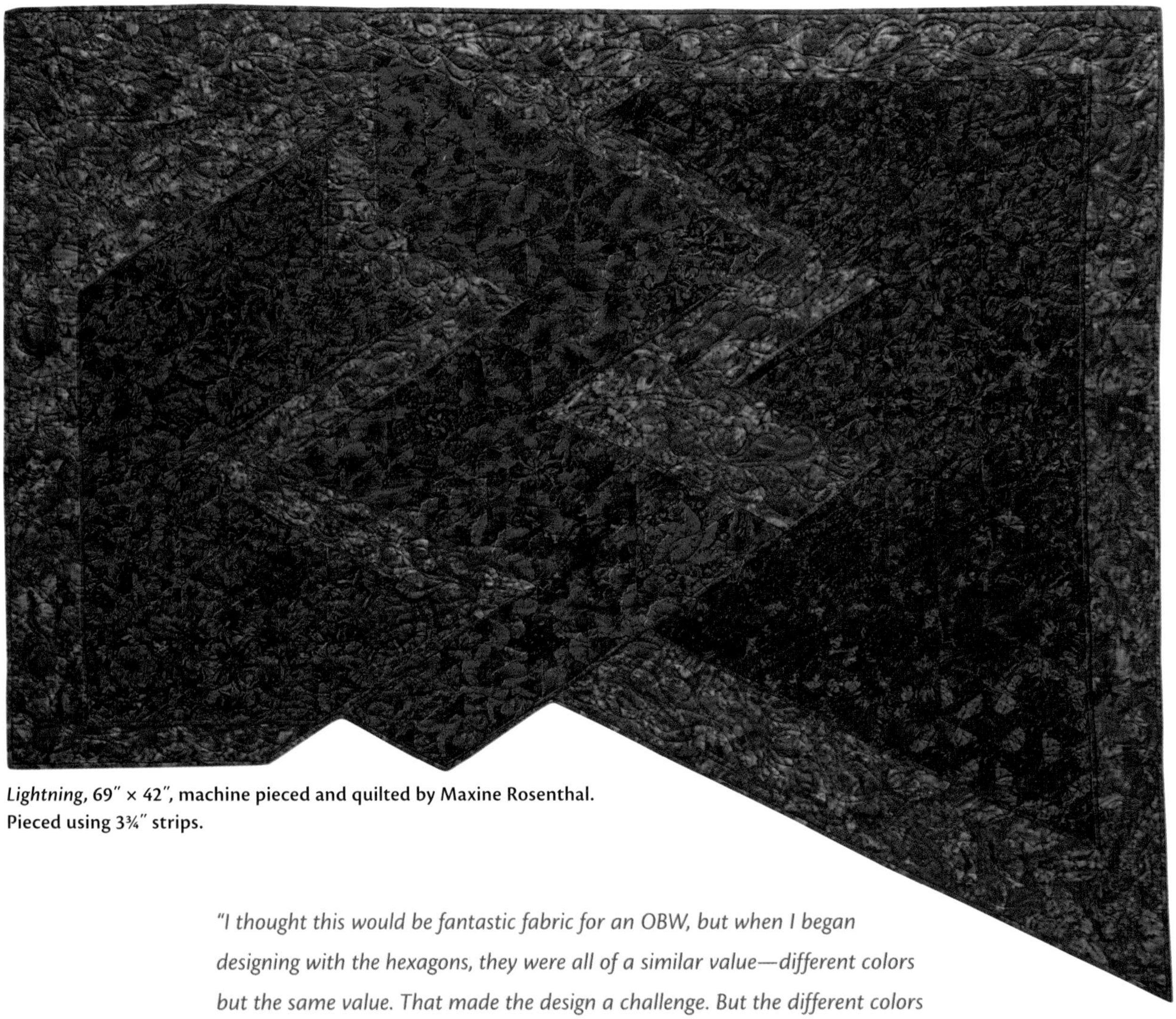

Lightning, 69″ × 42″, machine pieced and quilted by Maxine Rosenthal. Pieced using 3¾″ strips.

"I thought this would be fantastic fabric for an OBW, but when I began designing with the hexagons, they were all of a similar value—different colors but the same value. That made the design a challenge. But the different colors separated out so well, and the hexagons make that perfect 60° angle, so I just went with that."

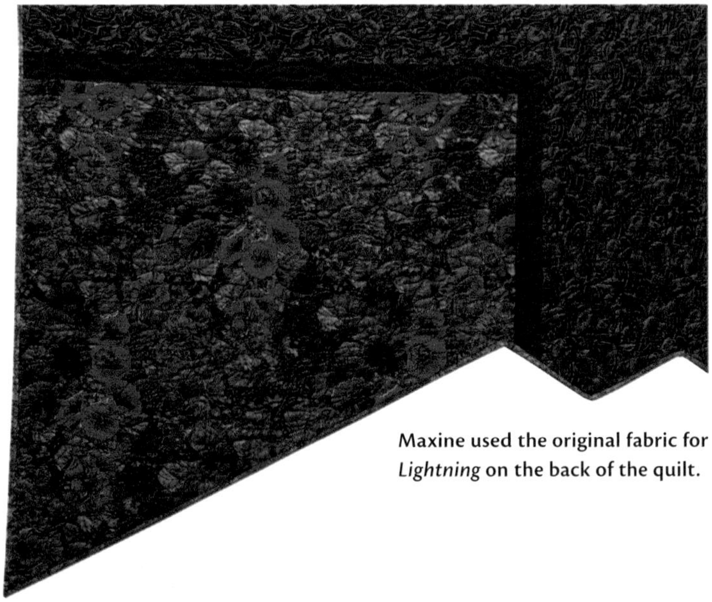

Maxine used the original fabric for *Lightning* on the back of the quilt.

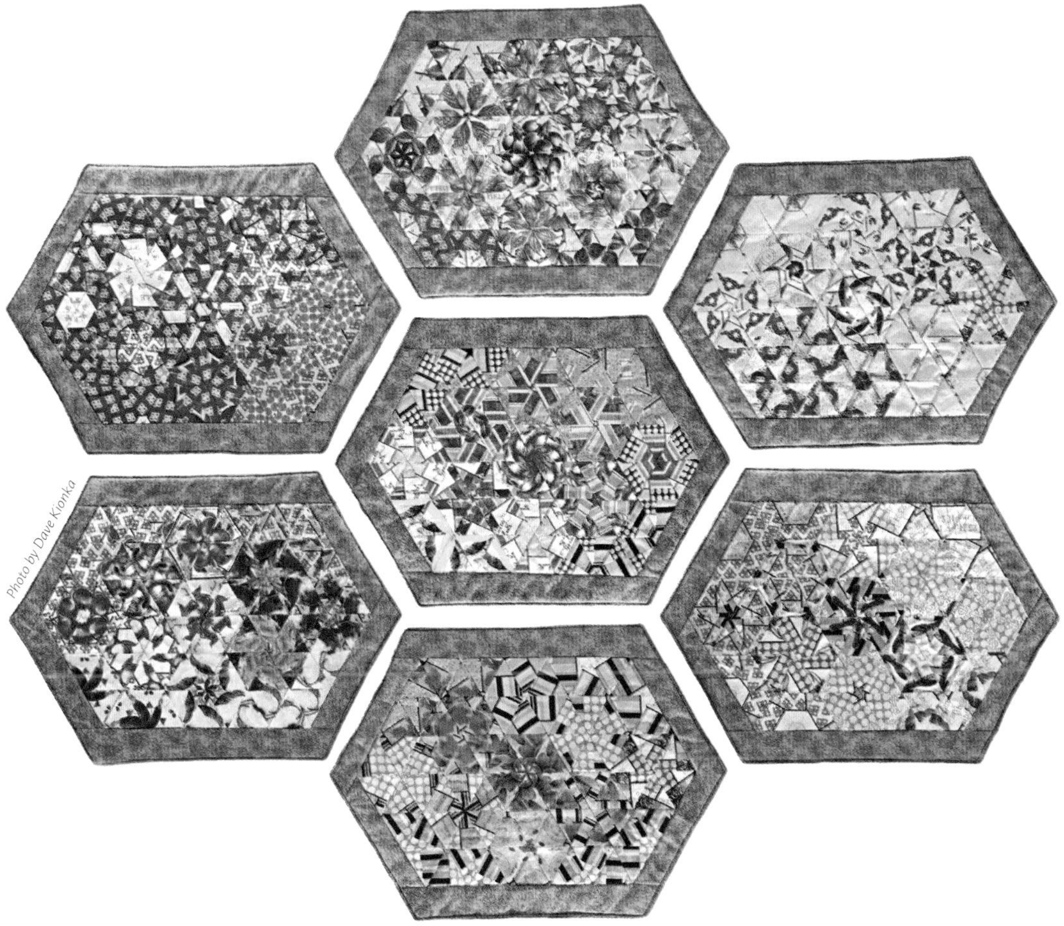

Simple Surprise place mats, 19″ × 13″, machine pieced and quilted by Ruth Ebert, 2015. Pieced using 2½″ strips.

"I bought a yard of this fabric before I had ever heard of One-Block Wonders. Once I discovered the technique, I was captivated by the possibilities and decided to experiment with this fabric before trying a full quilt. When I realized how small the repeat was and how little material I had, I decided to find the repeat both horizontally and vertically and cut strips in both directions to obtain the most possible variety in the resulting hexagons. I found the perfect green to tie the place mats together and complement my kitchen."

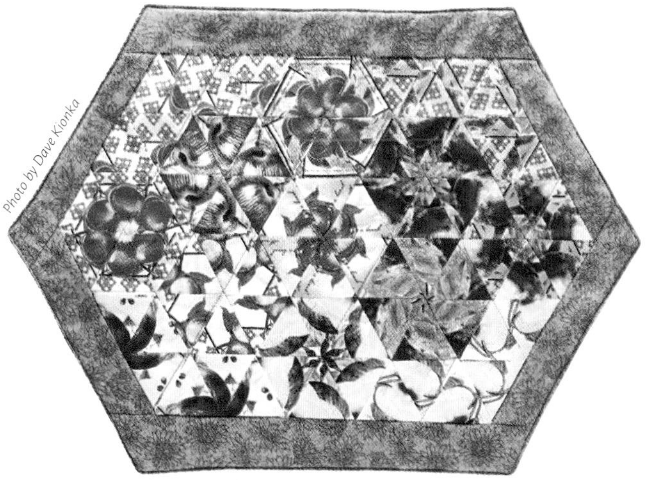

Close-up of a single place mat

Original fabric for Simple Surprise place mats. The repeat is 11″.

Japanese Tea Ceremony, 69″ × 83″, machine pieced and hand quilted by the women of Padukas, a women's art workshop in the outback of Mumbai, India. Designed by Asha Morei and Jeanetta Monosoff Haley. Pieced using 5½″ strips.

"Linda Bardes sent us One-Block Wonders as a gift. Our managers went to the wholesale scrap market in Mumbai and picked out fabric based on what they saw in the book. At first our women just followed with the pictures because they don't read English, and this resulted in some mistakes. Sanjana Garel was thoroughly taken with the idea and started making rows and rows of fabric, cutting them out one at a time. Once she realized she could layer them and cut multiple triangles at once, she enjoyed the process even more. We selected an antique Japanese quilt as the model for our layout."

CHAPTER 8

MOST FREQUENTLY ASKED QUESTIONS

WHY AREN'T MY CUBES THE SAME SIZE AS THE HEXAGONS?

MAXINE SAYS:

I have gotten many questions about why the cubes don't fit well and why they don't fit with the hexagons. The answer is always that the quiltmaker used a triangle ruler that does not have a top point. With a blunt-tip ruler, the triangles are cut ¼″ larger and with a 1½″ strip. This will never work.

A 3¾″ triangle divides perfectly into three equal parts, which is what the triangles for the cubes are made from: three strips of the same size. But if you used a ruler without a tip and didn't adjust the cutting line to 3½″, you essentially started with a 4″ triangle with the top missing—really a trapezoid—and it is next to impossible to divide 4″ into three equal parts with our rulers (refer to The Differences in 60° Rulers, page 9). Here are the instructions for using a blunt-tip ruler to make cubes that will match a kaleidoscopic hexagon that was cut with a blunt-tip ruler.

- Use strips that are 1⅝″ rather than 1½″.
- Cut the large trapezoids at the 3¾″ line.
- Cut the medium trapezoids on the 2¾″ line.
- Cut the small trapezoids on the 1¾″ line.

This will also work for the cubes that are opened on the sides and, of course, the cube in a cube or cube in the corner.

The original recipe for cubes is in *One-Block Wonders Encore!* (by C&T Publishing).

WHY AREN'T MY HEXAGONS ALL THE SAME SIZE?

LINDA SAYS:

Your ruler may have slipped as you cut your strips, which means that when you cut your triangles and sew them together, they will be different sizes. I have noticed that using a 60° triangle ruler gives me more accuracy.

WHY SHOULD I IRON MY SEAMS OPEN?

MAXINE SAYS:

It distributes the bulk. The upside of pressing seams to one side is that there is this wonderful thing that happens when a seam ironed one way fits in with a seam ironed the other way.

That is great, but with all these hexagons, which way would you iron? Ironing open means you don't have to think about which way.

DO I REALLY NEED TO KEEP THE POINTS?

LINDA SAYS:

No, but it makes it a lot easier to match triangles as you are sewing everything together. Not to mention that it is extra work and time-consuming to remove them.

WHY DON'T THE CENTERS OF MY HEXAGONS LIE FLAT?

LINDA SAYS:

One reason could be that the original strips, or the triangles cut from them, were not cut accurately. Most likely the ruler slipped; even a small difference will add up. After the half-hexagons are sewn into long strips and before the final assembly, check to see if there are any glaring wonky edges, and, if so, trim them straight. Though the center points of the hexagon will not match perfectly, no one will notice them in the overall finished quilt. See Chapter 3: Cutting and Sewing (page 19).

MAXINE SAYS:

Press the heck out of it.

CAN I ENTER MY QUILT IN A CONTEST?

MAXINE SAYS:

Yes, absolutely. This is a process, and you are the designer. Your quilt is a one of a kind.

HOW SHOULD I QUILT MY ONE-BLOCK WONDER?

MAXINE SAYS:

I have spent all my time designing the hexagons to a pleasing effect, and I do not want the quilting to overpower the design or be in competition with it. I want my fabric designing to be what is seen. I use a thread color that will blend into the fabric and as little quilting as I can get away with, in an allover pattern.

LINDA SAYS:

Keep in mind that if you heavily quilt your quilt, it will fight with the flow of the design you just created. You will also lose the overall dynamics of the quilt because it becomes about the quilting and not the quilt. As you may have noticed, however, some quilters have gotten good results with heavy quilting—especially in the borders. We tried to show some examples of quilting throughout the book.

On some of my quilts, especially if I consider the piece to be an art quilt to hang on the wall, I look for some fabric in my stash that I will never use and substitute it for batting. It gives the quilt a flat look, which is what I usually am looking for in a wallhanging, and it tends to hang better. It becomes more like a painting rather than a quilt.

In *Joy/Luck* (page 6), Linda Bardes quilted varying numbers of a concentric hexagons within many of the blocks and then stitched along the edge of the pinwheel designs in other pieced hexagons. The variation in texture adds movement to the subtle coloration.

In *Reef Hexed* (page 32) and *Under the Sea* (page 33), Kathy Gannon used a simple orange-peel quilting design to complement the blocks. It's just the right amount of quilting and leaves a lovely pattern on the back of the quilt.

Simple orange-peel quilting also worked for the hexagons in Liz Granberg's *Wanderlust: Paris in Spring* (page 67) and *Poppy Explosion* (page 29). In both quilts, Liz chose to quilt intricate designs in the original fabrics featured on the quilt tops. The closer, more detailed quilting on the original prints balances the busyness of the pieced hexagons.

Diana Eaton used different thread colors and heavy quilting to add diamonds to the border of *Nana's Flower Garden* (page 61).

Jackie O'Brien used light thread to quilt leafy designs into the dark, solid quilt border of *Just Lion Around* (page 62). For another example of Jackie's border quilting, see how she used light thread to enliven the border of *A Walk in Frida's Garden* (page 38).

DO I HAVE TO USE ALL OF THE HEXAGONS?

MAXINE SAYS:

This is your quilt; you don't "have to" do anything. I made a quilt and did not like any of the tan hexagons. I saved them and used them as pot holders to give as hostess gifts.

LINDA SAYS:

I like to put the extras on the back of the quilt. I have cut a few into squares and used them in the corners of the quilt. This way I have none left over. See *Birds in the Garden* (page 25).

For one of my quilts, however, I set myself the goal of using every hexagon on the front. The fabric—an Asian print—turned out to be a poor choice because it had a lot of open space without any interest and some big, colorful flowers with no background. I ended up with lots of plain-colored hexagons and lots of solid-colored hexagons. After several weeks and many attempts at a layout, I took it all down, and it's still under the bed.

CONTRIBUTORS

Photo by T. Dirk Wentling, CPP

BETTY BERG,
CONCORD, CALIFORNIA

Photo by Bart Huscher of About Faces Photography

SUE FENWICK,
SPRINGFIELD, MISSOURI

Photo by Stacey Cox

EMMA AND KAREN HUFMAN,
AGRICOLA, KANSAS

Photo by Cynthia Bosley

CYNTHIA BOSLEY,
TOLEDO, OHIO

Photo by Bill Krause

BARB FROST,
PITTSFORD, NEW YORK

Photo by Stephanie Strasner

JENELL HENNING,
LEXINGTON, OKLAHOMA

Photo by Kelly Bailey

SHARON H. LAKE,
SPRING LAKE, MICHIGAN

Photo by Tim Barnwell

JEAN CONDON,
ABINGDON, VIRGINIA

Photo by Kevin Gannon

KATHY GANNON,
ALBANY, NEW YORK

Photo by Lori Johnson

LORI JOHNSON,
REDDING, CALIFORNIA

Photo by Debbie Scott of Outback Pics

FAYE MCCARTHY,
BURNIE, TASMANIA, AUSTRALIA

Photo by Wayne Randall

DIANA EATON, MOLESWORTH,
TASMANIA, AUSTRALIA

Photo by Liz Granberg

LIZ GRANBERG (GYPSY DREAMER
QUILTS), BALDWIN CITY, KANSAS

Photo by René Hermans

HELENA KIESER,
CAPETOWN, SOUTH AFRICA

Photo by Harry Moos

SHARON MOOS,
CARMICHAEL, CALIFORNIA

Photo by Bill Ebert

RUTH EBERT,
WATERTOWN, WISCONSIN

Photo by Ada Bahlman

ELS HELLEMAN,
NETHERLANDS

Photo by Dick Kruse

JOAN KRUSE,
VADNAIS HEIGHTS, MINNESOTA

Photo by Lena R. Connor

VERLIE MURPHY,
SALUDA, NORTH CAROLINA

Photo by Vejay Gawi

PADUKAS WOMEN'S SEWING COOPERATIVE, OUTBACK OF MUMBAI, INDIA

Photo by Jackie O'Brien

JACKIE O'BRIEN, WHITESBORO, NEW YORK

Photo by Paul G. Sharpe

SUE SHARPE, LINDSAY, ONTARIO, CANADA

Photo by Ron Pearson

CHRIS PEARSON, SAN DIEGO, CALIFORNIA, AND LORETO, BAJA CALIFORNIA SUR, MEXICO

Photo by Doreen Stocker

MAY SMITH, OLYMPIA, WASHINGTON

Photo by Sam Tsiolis

DEBBIE PEEVER, ORLÉANS, ONTARIO, CANADA

Photo by Lisa Fritz of Camralynz Photography

DARLENE WILLIAMS, CLEBURNE, TEXAS

Photo by Grant Palmer

BRUCE SEEDS, MILWAUKEE, WISCONSIN

Photo by Valerie J. Todd

LINDA WILLIAMS, CLARKRIDGE, ARKANSAS

RESOURCES

Books and Tools

One-Block Wonders by Maxine Rosenthal (by C&T Publishing)

One-Block Wonders Encore! by Maxine Rosenthal and Joy Pelzmann (by C&T Publishing)

One-Block Wonders Cubed! by Maxine Rosenthal and Joy Pelzmann (by C&T Publishing)

Clearview Triangle 6″ Acrylic Ruler by Marci Baker

Padukas Quilt Cooperative

Padukas is a project of Shree Nityananda Education Trust (SNET), whose mission is to improve the lifestyle of impoverished women living in rural India by teaching them new skills and giving them employment opportunities. The cooperative is located 2 hours north of Mumbai, India. Tribal women there live in poverty, without modern comforts. Padukas has over 28 women working 6 to 7 hours a day. This allows them to still have time to tend to their family's needs of gathering water at the well (up to 8 trips a day), gathering firewood, and cooking over a woodstove.

SNET is changing lives for young women by making it possible for them to avoid early marriage and its disastrous health effects; teaching them to read and write in their native language, during work hours; creating income opportunities for women to help them provide better nutrition and education for their families; and helping develop confidence, creativity, and new skills in a male-dominated culture.

Visit Padukas Quilt Cooperative online:

Website: padukaseboutique.com

Etsy shop: etsy.com/shop/Padukas

ABOUT THE AUTHORS

Maxine Rosenthal started quilting almost 40 years ago (my, how time flies!). She belonged to the Minnesota Quilters, and they were kind enough to allow her to enter her first quilt in their annual show.

She was so excited that she told her daughter to look around and find something she liked; Maxine would make it for her. Her daughter picked a kaleidoscopic quilt ("And make it in pink and purple, please?"). Well a promise is a promise, so Maxine first had to learn what it meant to work with kaleidoscopic blocks. Pink and purple? Never going to happen. Instead she found a green floral fabric with some pink and purple. She started by cutting a piece of plastic template material and placing it on the fabric, drawing the design on the template, and then using that to cut 8 identical diamonds. She made that quilt for her daughter's ninth birthday. Her daughter is now 37 and has many, many quilts—all kaleidoscopic, and yes, she still has that very first one.

Maxine loved all the kaleidoscopic blocks but did not like that they were separate from each other, like bull's-eyes on a background. How could they be placed without background fabric? Hexagons are shaped exactly like beehives, which have no spaces. The idea took hold.

The notion that one fabric produces such diverse kaleidoscopic effects is what has kept Maxine making these quilts for almost 30 years.

Photo by Olan Mills

Linda Bardes has sewn most of her life, making clothes for herself, her children, and family. When her children (two boys and two girls) were little, there was a Munsingwear fabric outlet where she could buy yards of underwear fabric, elastic, nylon, and lace for nightgowns, as well as fabric for the more formal T-shirts with collars. Until her children started school, she sewed everything but their socks. She made nightgowns and peignoir sets for herself and as gifts.

One year she went off in an old van she called Poor Butterfly and toted her sewing machine around the country. She bartered her sewing for unoccupied resort rooms. In one small resort on the waterfront in Provincetown, Massachusetts, she mended canvas canopies.

Linda admits to looking for new and unusual ways to do almost everything. She refers to this as her personality quirk that sometimes makes life harder than it needs to be. As a result, she was primed to jump headfirst into the One-Block Wonder process when she discovered it. She admits to being a novice quilter who could not sew a point without a square end, but OBWs don't present that problem (and when they do, no one notices).

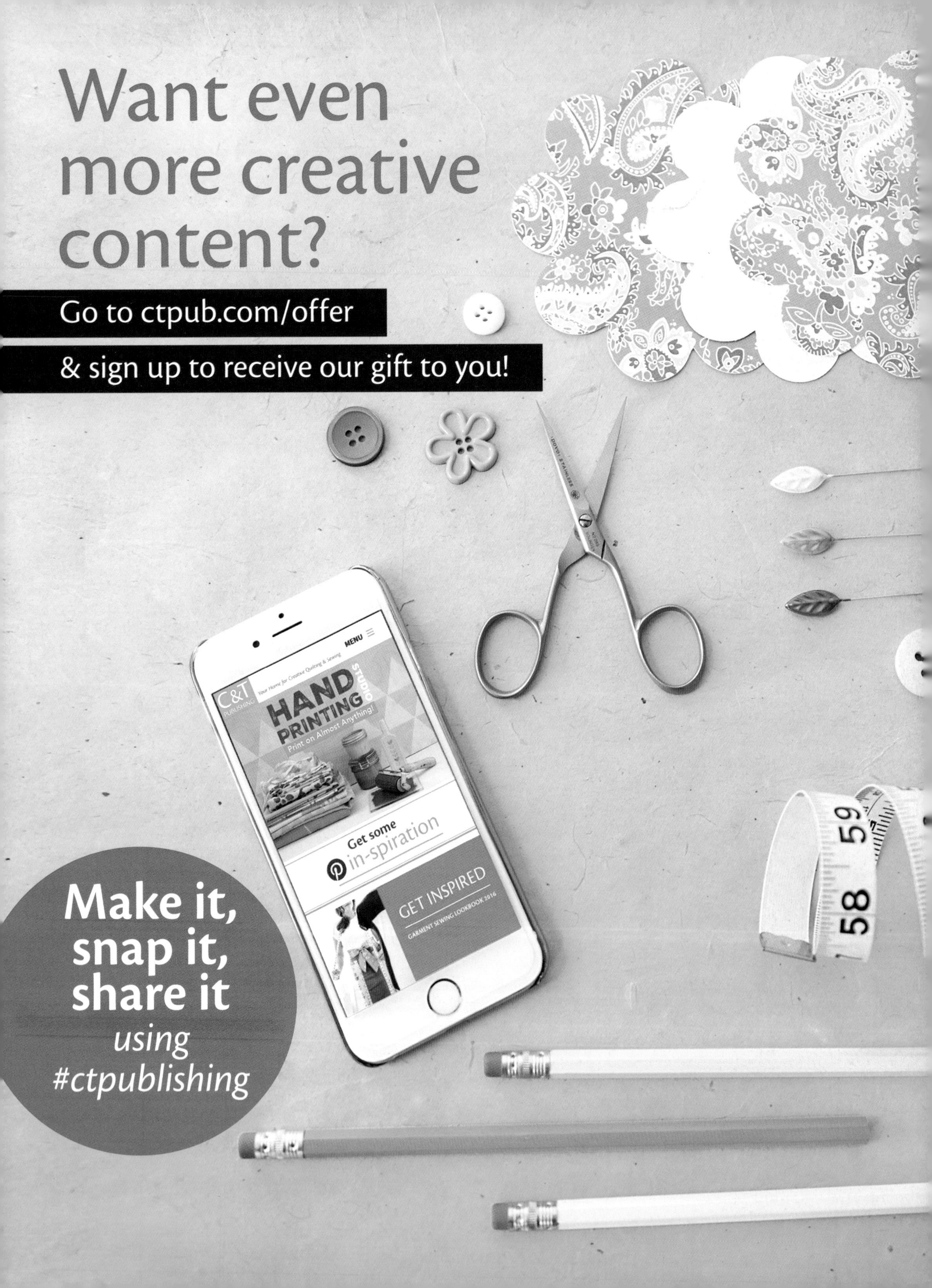

Want even more creative content?
Go to ctpub.com/offer
& sign up to receive our gift to you!
MENU
C&T PUBLISHING
Your Home for Creative Quilting & Sewing
HAND PRINTING STUDIO
Print on Almost Anything!
Get some in-spiration
GET INSPIRED
GARMENT SEWING LOOKBOOK 2016
Make it, snap it, share it using #ctpublishing